Praise for
The Busy Mom's Devotional

"I absolutely love this devotional! It is deep, yet doable; rich, yet practical—
the perfect place to start (or continue!) a lifelong pursuit of God."

—JOANNA WEAVER, best-selling author of *Having a Mary Heart*
in a Martha World and *Having a Mary Spirit*

"Lisa's tender heart for the Lord shines on every page. Each reflection feels
like an invitation to trust Christ even more with all the details of life. I
love the way Lisa's personal stories amplify the truths found in the daily
Scripture verses."

—ROBIN JONES GUNN, best-selling novelist and author of *Take*
Flight! A Sisterchicks Devotional

"Whether tackling potty training or driver's training, busy moms of all
ages and stages will unearth timeless treasures on every page of this book!
Lisa's relevant stories and rejuvenating scriptures provide rest stops of
refuge for maxed-out moms as they seek to reconnect with their Creator
in the midst of their hectic week."

—KAREN EHMAN, author of *A Life That Says Welcome,* national
speaker for Hearts at Home and Proverbs 31 Ministries, and a
homeschooling mother of three

The
BUSY Mom's
devotional

ALSO BY LISA T. BERGREN

FICTION
The Begotten
The Betrayed
The Bridge
Christmas Every Morning
The Captain's Bride
Deep Harbor
Midnight Sun

CHILDREN'S BOOKS
God Gave Us You
God Gave Us Two
God Gave Us Christmas
How Big Is God?

The
BUSY Mom's
devotional

10 Minutes a Week
to a Life of Devotion

Lisa T. Bergren

WATERBROOK
PRESS

THE BUSY MOM'S DEVOTIONAL
PUBLISHED BY WATERBROOK PRESS
12265 Oracle Boulevard, Suite 200
Colorado Springs, Colorado 80921

Details in some anecdotes and stories have been changed to protect the identities of the
persons involved.

ISBN 978-1-4000-7246-0

Published in the United States by WaterBrook Multnomah, an imprint of the Crown Pub-
lishing Group, a division of Random House Inc., New York.

WATERBROOK and its deer colophon are registered trademarks of Random House Inc.

Library of Congress Cataloging-in-Publication Data
Bergren, Lisa Tawn.
    The busy mom's devotional : ten minutes a week to a life of devotion / Lisa T. Bergren.
— 1st ed.
        p. cm.
    Includes bibliographical references and index.
    ISBN 978-1-4000-7246-0
    1. Mothers—Prayers and devotions. 2. Christian women—Prayers and devotions.
I. Title.
    BV4847.B44 2007
    242'.6431—dc22

                                                    2007006000

Printed in the United States of America
2015

10 9 8 7 6

For Mom,
who, in the midst of all her own busyness,
always made me feel loved, respected, encouraged, and accepted.
I love you!

Contents

Introduction

Dear Friends,
You're reading this with some sense of skepticism. How can you, one of the world's busiest moms, running about every day of your life with a thousand things to do, have a devotional life?

I know that's what you're asking because I've done the same. Some days it seems impossible. Hey, my entire life seems impossible on certain days.

But the truth is, the devotional life is more a *way* of looking at your life than anything you *do*. It's beginning to see God infusing every moment of your day. Examples may be watching *Lion King* and seeing Jesus imagery in Simba, or considering how God keeps a hold on us just as our children seem to have suction cups on their arms and legs that are impossible to dislodge, or thinking how God watches over us just as we watch over our children and gaze at them in pleasure as they breathe softly in and out.

There is a bit of mind and heart training to be done in order to see such things. But it's worth the time and energy, because, I promise you, this new perspective will add a depth and dimension to your life that you've never experienced before. Instead of feeling like your days are one long to-do list, you'll begin to notice small treasures along the way. Life will seem richer, more important. Mundane tasks can take on epic importance as we understand that our little lives are part of a much greater story—a story of good versus evil. *And each day and each life counts. Your* day, your life counts.

Over the course of the next year, you'll see glimpses into my mind and heart, those times when I noticed God and took the time to write it down. Nothing is keeping you from doing the very same thing. All you have to do is put on your "Jesus glasses" so you can see Him everywhere you look and then take a moment to journal what you see.

So, friend, I beg you to begin. For you. For your children (because what you learn, they will learn eventually too).

Declare Thursday mornings or Sunday afternoons or Monday nights—whenever you can carve out five to fifteen minutes—as your time, and write "Mom's Break" on your calendar. Don't let anything displace this time, or if it does get displaced, pick up that time later by getting up just a bit earlier. Enlist your husband (and your children if they're old enough) to help you stick with this endeavor to know God better. How can they refuse? And what better example could you set for them than to show you care about your relationship with God?

In five minutes you can read each week's devotional and pray. In ten to fifteen minutes, you can go further, making the truth yours by using surprisingly simple, ancient Christian practices. Just five to fifteen minutes! (An average of ten minutes gave us our subtitle—there's freedom and flexibility here. No stress!) You'll find prompts in each chapter to help:

- **Things on My Mind:** Do this before you even begin reading. In order to focus, we busy moms have to get our lists or things we're fretting about—*whatever* it is—down on paper so we can concentrate. Therefore, take note: *you are to write in this book.* Anywhere you wish! (Umm...unless it's a library book!)
- **What Is God Saying to Me in This?** is for you to write any questions, responses, or thoughts you have about what you've just read. Allow yourself to react here so your honest feelings will emerge; you can contemplate all this more in moments that follow.

- **Making the Scripture Mine** reexamines the scripture related to the chapter's message and helps you apply it to the moment.
- **My Prayer** is for you to write your own prayer. Even people who don't think of themselves as writers find that a pencil or pen in hand helps keep them focused in prayer when they might otherwise be distracted. Jot down notes, phrases, words—whatever— knowing that the Holy Spirit will make up the difference.

Do you see how these prompts move you from listening and absorbing to interacting with God and then applying His Word and will to your mind and heart?

If you'd rather, you can use this as a daily devotional for a month or two. Just don't get overwhelmed and quit. Take on what you can and stick with it. It may take you eighteen months to read it. That is perfectly fine. Don't fret about it. Make it a *gift of time* versus another *guilt-inducing "to do"* in your life. Remember, we're gently retraining our brains and hearts so we may become women who live a life of devotion. That takes time…and a healthy measure of grace. God offers us both. Don't refuse either the gift or the invitation!

You're about to turn the page and enter the devotional life. You. Crazy, busy you. Jesus longs to walk beside you, day in and day out. Can you see Him there beside you, smiling?

Your sister along the road,

Lisa Bergren

P.S. We've arranged the devotionals to fit in a specific season rather than to follow a chronological order, so please ignore references to my children's ages or grades that are at times out of order.

Part 1

Winter

Core Work

That's why, when I heard of the solid trust you have in the Master Jesus and your outpouring of love to all the Christians, I couldn't stop thanking God for you—every time I prayed, I'd think of you and give thanks. But I do more than thank. I ask—ask the God of our Master, Jesus Christ, the God of glory—to make you intelligent and discerning in knowing him personally, your eyes focused and clear, so that you can see exactly what it is he is calling you to do, grasp the immensity of this glorious way of life he has for Christians, oh, the utter extravagance of his work in us who trust him—endless energy, boundless strength!

All this energy issues from Christ: God raised him from death and set him on a throne in deep heaven, in charge of running the universe, everything from galaxies to governments, no name and no power exempt from his rule. And not just for the time being, but *forever.*

EPHESIANS 1:15–21

Things on My Mind

Concerns, to-do lists, grocery lists, whatever—get these things down here so you can concentrate for the next ten minutes.

_____

_____

_____

I'm trying to lose thirty pounds. I'm down about ten, with twenty to go, and I know I'll get stuck in another five or so. All my life I've seemed to carry an extra fifteen pounds. But I have a new passion: Jazzercise. A young woman started a class just around the block from me, making it hard for me to claim it's too tough to get there. So I'm going, hoping it will help me reach that fifteen-pound marker and beyond.

One of the things I like is that I'm toning muscles. Three babies and fifteen years behind a computer have left me…um…unmuscled. So Michelle, my Jazzercise instructor, is teaching me how to lift resistance weights, and she's doing it in a way I've never tried before.

If you're a part of the exercise world at all, you've undoubtedly heard of core work. While I've read about this in magazines and been told I need to do it by a good friend who has done it and benefited, I never have tried it. If you, like me, breeze over those magazine articles to avoid one more bit of guilt in your life, I understand.

But core work is helping me. It's strengthening all the muscles in my torso so I am more balanced, stronger. We've been doing lifts where you raise one arm and the opposite leg and hold it in T formation. (Try that at home if you want to get a sense of core work.) At first I couldn't hold it. I was off balance. But more and more I'm able to hold it, switch positions, and then hold it again. I'm getting better at finding the center of me, the place where gravity pulls me down the strongest, and concentrating on that helps me forget how heavy a limb can be.

I think God is calling us to enter into some core work with Him. To center on what we know is truth, on scriptures that edify and encourage and shape us. To walk in the light rather than wallow in the dark. When women cry out for balance in their lives, I think this is a big part of it.

Core work with Jesus brings us balance. Core work means remembering (a) we were created for a purpose; (b) we are unconditionally loved; (c) our sins are forgiven and forgotten; (d) Christ wants the very best for us, day in and day out; and (e) Christ wants us to know Him better and live for Him. When we concentrate on those things, we can shed the distractions that keep us from the balance we crave.

Spiritual core work helps us filter the things that come flying at us every day—shame, fear, anger, commitments, demands, pressure—and siphon away the things that don't support a, b, c, d, or e. We can say no to the wrong things, yes to the right ones. And the more spiritually muscled we get, the better we move, feel, and believe we can do.

Savior, I want to be strong in You. There's so much in this world that pulls at me, bringing me down, leaving me misshapen, not the creation You see in me. Help me get stronger in the truths I know already and those You have yet to teach me. Help me stand taller for You. It's in Your name I pray. Amen.

What Is God Saying to Me in This?

_____

_____

_____

Making the Scripture Mine

Paul had spent several years in Ephesus, helping believers there gain a solid foundation. And unlike other letters in which he addresses particular problems or heresies, in Ephesians he teaches about the broad horizons, the grand expanse of God, and His high goals for each of us. In this passage Paul teaches that the source of strength that resides in us is the same power that raised Jesus from the dead—the Holy Spirit.

Read Ephesians 1:15–21 (at the beginning of this devotional from The Message, or in your own Bible) again slowly, as if you were opening the letter from Paul and needed to read it to others. How would you reword the scripture for your circumstances? Or is this exactly what you need to hear, as it's written? If so, comment on why it speaks to you.

Pray, "Father, show me what You want me to learn in this passage." Now reread the verses and finish this sentence: God wants me to...

My Prayer

Baby Steps for a New Year

I remember it all—oh, how well I remember—
the feeling of hitting the bottom.
But there's one other thing I remember,
and remembering, I keep a grip on hope:
GOD's loyal love couldn't have run out,
his merciful love couldn't have dried up.
They're created new every morning.
How great your faithfulness!

LAMENTATIONS 3:20–23

I love the start of a new year. At the beginning, I think all things are possible. I can be a better mom, a better wife, a better friend. I can obtain a new body (or maybe just a slightly modified version). I can exercise. I can learn something new every week. I can explore and sing and take time for small things that otherwise might get passed over. I can learn more about Jesus and become a better disciple.

> ### Things on My Mind
>
> Concerns, to-do lists, grocery lists, whatever—get these things down here so you can concentrate for the next ten minutes.
>
> _____
> _____
> _____

What is it about us or life that beats that hope out of us as the year progresses? Why is it that, come March or April, we've given up on our hopes for the new year and have settled into our comfortable, humdrum visions that we had last November? Why have we given into despair? or hopelessness? Why can we not hold on to this New Year's hope, this vision, the whole year through?

God does. He holds tight to the New Year's dream. To Him, we are new every morning, a New Year's package, waiting to be opened. To Him, every time we ask for forgiveness, we are new creatures, clean slates. All the baggage and strikes against us are gone, gone, gone, and we are like little children—full of hope and potential.

My friend Carolyn Arends performs an older song in which she sings, "Every day is New Year's Day." I think if we could hold on to the hope and set baby goals rather than radical goals (ten pounds versus thirty, one six-week Bible study rather than tackling the whole Bible, and so on), we would have a chance to make this new year something phenomenal. If only we could cling to the truth of God's faithfulness, to His desire to see us succeed! Climbing a mountain requires our placing one foot in front of the other. And getting up when we fall, eyes on the peak, and doing it again.

Father of Hope, I get ahead of myself. My dreams and visions and desires are big, big, big. Help me break them down into small steps. Help me celebrate small victories, knowing they are getting me closer to the goal: You and Your vision for my life. Amen.

What Is God Saying to Me in This?

_____

_____

_____

Making the Scripture Mine

Exodus is the Jews' glory story of deliverance; Lamentations is the story of their suffering in exile. Life was hard for these people—I mean *really* hard. We have no comprehension of it. Imagine wholesale slaughter in our streets, pastors being killed in our churches, starving mothers eating their children—this is the grim reality of Lamentations. But while most of us will never see such horror, all Scripture has relevance and meaning for us.

Read Lamentations 3:20–23 again slowly, as if the author of Lamentations were writing to you alone, in this day, in this place, seeing you in your private struggle. How would you reword the passage in the context of your circumstances today?

_____

_____

_____

Pray, "Father, show me what You want me to learn in this passage." Now reread the verses and finish this sentence: God wants me to...

_____

_____

_____

My Prayer

_____

_____

_____

Eyes in the Back of Our Heads

God is strong, and he wants you strong. So take everything the Master has set out for you, well-made weapons of the best materials. And put them to use so you will be able to stand up to everything the Devil throws your way.... This is for keeps, a life-or-death fight to the finish against the Devil and all his angels....

Take all the help you can get, every weapon God has issued, so that when it's all over but the shouting you'll still be on your feet. Truth, righteousness, peace, faith, and salvation are more than words. Learn how to apply them.... God's Word is an *indispensable* weapon. In the same way, prayer is essential in this ongoing warfare.... Keep your eyes open.

EPHESIANS 6:10–18

Things on My Mind

Concerns, to-do lists, grocery lists, whatever—get these things down here so you can concentrate for the next ten minutes.

_____

_____

_____

Last week I was told a mesmerizing story about Bengal tigers and their caretakers on a preserve in India. Before the preserve was in place, the Bengal tiger was endangered and had dwindled to a frightening few in this remote part of India.

But given time and protection, the tigers made a comeback, gradually increasing in numbers. The disturbing thing was that, as their numbers increased, the people who protected them were dwindling in greater numbers. The Bengal tiger turned out to be a gifted hunter and, unable to discern between prey and protector, was eating his protectors left and right.

The people learned quickly that if the tiger thought they were watching, it would not attack. It only attacked from the back and only took down those who never looked around or behind them.

The guards on that Bengal tiger preserve came up with an ingenious plan. They wore masks that made them appear to have a face on the back of their heads. Therefore the tigers thought the guards were always on the lookout, always aware, and never safe to attack.

Suddenly the number of caretakers increased and made their own comeback from the endangered species list!

How can we, like the caretakers, be more vigilant on our watch for the enemy? How can we ward off Satan's attack on our hearts, our minds, our souls before he's upon us? By protecting ourselves. By clothing ourselves in the Word, arming ourselves with the Spirit, and being aware. Too often Satan catches us unaware. Too often we grow distracted, absorbed in our circumstances, and he uses that moment to pounce.

Paul begs us to fight to the finish, to ward off the Enemy by using the tools the Lord gave us. Take up your swords, sisters. Be vigilant. The battle is far from over.

Lord, thank You for protecting me. Help me be a wise follower, using all the tools You've given me to protect myself. Help me be vigilant, aware of the sin that tries to creep up on me, take me down. Help me fend it off and keep it far away from my heart, mind, and soul at all times. Lord God, make up the difference when I am weak. Sustain me and keep me. Place Your angels on guard all around me. I pray this in the name of the Lord Jesus Christ. Amen.

What Is God Saying to Me in This?

_____

_____

Making the Scripture Mine

Are you a realist? Do you have difficulty buying into science fiction or fantasy? Then I'm pretty sure you're struggling with these verses. Here Paul goes "cosmic," reminding us that every detail of our lives counts, that we're all part of a divine, epic drama, a story that will not end until the end of the age. So suspend disbelief for a moment, and read Ephesians 6:10–18 again slowly, as if you were opening up an urgent missive from a front-line commander. Now put key phrases from the scripture in your own words and in the context of your everyday life:

_____

_____

_____

Pray, "Father, show me what You want me to learn in this passage." Now reread the verses and finish this sentence: God wants me to…

_____

_____

_____

My Prayer

_____

_____

_____

Chocolate Intensity Prayer

The Jews, circling him, said, "How long are you going to keep us guessing? If you're the Messiah, tell us straight out."

Jesus answered, "I told you, but you don't believe. Everything I have done has been authorized by my Father, actions that speak louder than words. You don't believe because you're not my sheep. My sheep recognize my voice. I know them, and they follow me. I give them real and eternal life. They are protected from the Destroyer for good. No one can steal them from out of my hand."

JOHN 10:24–28

O ver Christmas break my household was a tad crazy. I was finishing a novel, doing my part in my book business, wrapping presents, cooking, baking, shopping, planning. My two-year-old followed me around one afternoon, asking for one thing or another. I was irritable and short, trying again and again to plant him in front of the television so I could get something done! (I know, Bad Mommy.)

He kept following me around, asking a question I couldn't understand,

> ### Things on My Mind
>
> Concerns, to-do lists, grocery lists, whatever—get these things down here so you can concentrate for the next ten minutes.
>
> _____
>
> _____
>
> _____

so I picked him up, sighed, and said, "What? What do you need, Jack?"

He took my face between his hands and got an inch away from it. "Mama, I *need* chocwate."

I laughed and gave in, of course, because he was so darn cute. I was half-amused, half-amazed that I couldn't make out his words before that moment. Where had my head been? His words were clear enough; I just wasn't really listening. It reminded me of how my friend Rebecca often prays that God will take our faces between His hands and make us look at Him.

When I discipline Jack, I often hold his face so he has to meet my gaze. His big brown eyes cast left and right in a desperate attempt to avoid eye contact. But when he wants chocolate, then he's the one forcing me to look at him!

Isn't this how we talk to God? When we want something, we jump up and down, yelling, screaming, wailing, gnashing our teeth. "God! Over here! Look at me! Do You hear me? I need this! God! Are You there?"

But when God has something to say to us? We too often turn away, run away. When He grabs hold of our faces, intent that we listen to Him, we look wildly left and right—anything to avoid hearing what our Papa has to say.

We are a fiercely independent people. God loves that about us; He does. It makes our love for Him all the more the prize He seeks. But I'm striving to submit to His hands upon my cheeks. To wait and hear what my Savior wants me to do. To keep my eyes on Him, steady, waiting for Him to speak, despite the distractions and internal desires that take me elsewhere. I want Him to speak to me with Jack's chocolate-desire intensity, and I want to hear and learn and believe.

Place Your hands on my cheeks, Father. Make me look to You when I get so wild and strung out. Make me hear Your voice above all others. Make me feel Your breath upon my face, giving me life when I feel drained. I want to be Your submissive child, Lord, a daughter who does as You bid. Forgive me for walking paths that do not honor You. Forgive me for speaking words You did not give me to speak. Forgive me for not keeping my eyes on You. I'm looking for You, Jesus. Reach for me, Lord. Hold me tight. Speak to me, and I will listen. Amen.

What Is God Saying to Me in This?

_____

_____

_____

Making the Scripture Mine

The apostle John was a pastor to a church (or churches), and in his letters he focused on three things: Jesus the Messiah is the center of everything; Jesus shows us everything we need to know about God; Jesus shows us how to love—and love fully. In John's ministry, he had trouble getting people focused on Jesus; they wanted to "make up their own idea of God...their own style of love.... In his letters we see him reestablishing the original and organic unity of God and love that comes to focus and becomes available to us in Jesus Christ."[1]

Read John 10:24–28 again slowly, as if you were hearing Jesus speak to you alone. What phrases speak the loudest to you today?

_____

_____

_____

Pray, "Father, show me what You want me to learn in this passage." Now reread the verses and finish this sentence: God wants me to...

_____

_____

_____

My Prayer

_____

_____

_____

_____

_____

_____

Fading Castles

"Now I'm stepping in," GOD says.
"From now on, I'm taking over.
The gloves come off. Now see how mighty I am.
There's nothing to you.
Pregnant with chaff, you produce straw babies;
full of hot air, you self-destruct.
You're good for nothing but fertilizer and fuel.
Earth to earth—and the sooner the better....
The sinners in Zion are rightly terrified;
the godless are at their wit's end:
'Who among us can survive this
　　firestorm?
Who of us can get out of this purge
　　with our lives?'"
The answer's simple:
Live right,
speak the truth,
despise exploitation,
refuse bribes,
reject violence,
avoid evil amusements.
This is how you raise your standard
　　of living!
A safe and stable way to live.
A nourishing, satisfying way to live.
　　　ISAIAH 33:10–16

Things on My Mind

Concerns, to-do lists, grocery lists, whatever—get these things down here so you can concentrate for the next ten minutes.

_____

_____

_____

O n a dream trip through Italy with my husband and our friends, we rented the most amazing farmhouse for the week. We were told the people who once lived in this farmhouse worked in the castle above, which immediately piqued our interest.

On the last morning of our stay, we decided to rise and hike, to see what we could see. The road was winding and long, and we climbed on and on—much higher than I ever imagined the hills of Tuscany would be.

The higher we went, the more we could see of the incredible Arezzo valley, her shoulders rising on either side, her belly bustling with industry. On the far side of the valley were the hills of the Chianti region, where buildings were sparser, and vineyards fought their way out of dense forests. On our side, it was a bit lighter. There were more olive groves and vineyards and townspeople than trees on our hills.

After much huffing and puffing, we reached the top and found the castle ruins but were disappointed that there are no turrets, no impressive ground floor. It is rather small and tidy—at least what remains. Perhaps it once boasted towers high above and outbuildings all around, but now it looks like simple, crumbling stone walls, with timbers rotting within.

It's when we looked out to the valley that we saw a view fit for princes, a view worthy of a castle. From this vantage point, its owners once could have seen enemy Florentine troops riding toward them. They would have been able to see traders and pilgrims on their way to Rome. They would have been able to see their olive groves and vineyards and fields everywhere they looked.

I wonder what it felt like to live in that castle, to command such a region, to own such a place on earth. My mind ambles toward the romantic vision, but I assume it was more cold and drafty than I can even imagine. Keeping all they had amassed was obviously a difficult enterprise. What brought about their demise? Poor management? Poor choices? Evil doing? God does not suffer an unrighteous man (or woman) for long.

Perhaps slowly the vineyards and fields had to be sold off. Perhaps the olive groves, closest to the castle, were the last to go. When did the castle begin to fail? When was it that the mason could not be called for repairs? How many winters did they endure without wood in the fireplace to warm them?

As Christmas fades and the new year flourishes, I want to focus more on Christ than on my stuff or things I want. I don't want to dream of fairy-tale fortunes or bigger houses or more clothes or a new car. I don't want to be distracted by schemes on how to get ahead in our temporal world.

I want to think about my faith and how I can grow in my discipleship, to become a woman God praises in the heavens. I want to squeeze the Bible for knowledge, just as they squeeze the olives in Italy, and pour Scripture, like the finest of oils, through my mind and heart. Ninety-nine percent of grand castles no longer look so awe inspiring. But Jesus? The God Baby who comes for us again and again? He looks more grand by the day.

I don't know what's wrong with me, Lord. Over and over I learn the difference between what I want and what I need, but still I fall back into my I-want-I-want-I-want rut. I get distracted by pressures, people, misplaced priorities. Please teach me to see as You see, to think as You think. Help me cast away frivolous desires and conquer sin and greed on a daily basis. I am weak. Help me want You in my life more than anything else. Because You are my Always and Forever. Amen.

What Is God Saying to Me in This?

_____

_____

_____

Making the Scripture Mine

Isaiah speaks of the coming judgment of the Lord in this passage. How vain we are, trying to build our fortresses as if we could be mighty enough to become our own power in the world. Read Isaiah 33:10–16 again slowly, as if you could literally hear God's voice booming these words to you (or is He whispering?). Now, how would you restate the passage in your own words and everyday context?

_____

_____

_____

Pray, "Father, show me what You want me to learn in this passage." Now reread the verses and finish this sentence: God wants me to...

_____

_____

_____

My Prayer

_____

_____

_____

Looking for the Sun

> You're here to be light, bringing out the God-colors in the world. God is not a secret to be kept. We're going public with this, as public as a city on a hill. If I make you light-bearers, you don't think I'm going to hide you under a bucket, do you? I'm putting you on a light stand. Now that I've put you there on a hilltop, on a light stand—shine!
>
> MATTHEW 5:14–16

These verses remind me of the kids' song "This Little Light of Mine." I'd like to think that I always let my light shine, but sometimes it gets choked, like a candle flame without oxygen. Sometimes it's by things around me, sometimes by things within.

My friend Jenny lives in Arizona now, but at one time she lived in the Midwest. She says there was a stretch of twenty-one days when no sun emerged. Dark rain clouds covered the sky, locking out all light. It was the kind of weather that makes you want to lean toward the windows while you do dishes to absorb at least a smidgen of vitamin D. It was the kind of weather that makes you wonder if you have SAD and need to wear a headlamp.

Things on My Mind

Concerns, to-do lists, grocery lists, whatever—get these things down here so you can concentrate for the next ten minutes.

Jenny has a dear friend who lived next door to her at the time, an artist who paints in bold strokes and colors, with wide-open, curving, welcoming lines. During those twenty-one days of dismal, dark weather, she sat down at the canvas and intentionally chose bright, sunny shades of gold and orange, spring green and summer blue. Through her painting, through a conscious choice, she got her dose of vitamin D and escaped the dismal effects of the weather.

I want to be like Jenny's artist friend. When life seems too gray—when all I want to do is climb back into bed—I want to find my own sunny outlet. Chuck Swindoll says the most important choice you make each day is what your attitude will be. And I find that's true. Every day I can be at peace or stressed, happy or grumpy. No matter how bad the day, there is *always* something in my life I can be thankful for, something I can choose to dwell on that brings me joy. I can choose to look for the sun instead of getting overwhelmed by the gray. When I choose the Son, I reflect His light instead of absorbing a tank full of dark. And that's when I shine brightest.

Jesus, help me remember that attitude is a choice. Help me choose to look for the good in each day, to seek Your light when all seems dark. Thank You for always being present for me, for being my sun in every day. Amen.

What Is God Saying to Me in This?

_____

_____

_____

Making the Scripture Mine

To put Matthew 5:14–16 in context, think back to Jesus' day, to how dark night was without electricity. Their lamps were small oil lamps with one tiny flame. To get a sense of that, this evening you might light a few candles around your house and turn off all your light fixtures. How much light is there? How dark is it? This was Jesus' reference when He said these words. He knew that we'd be but one miserable, sputtering candle. Yet Jesus said we're supposed to be the "light of the world." How do you make sense of that?

Read the passage again slowly, as if you were listening to Jesus speak to you. How would you reword the scripture for your own life? Start by inserting your name, as in "Lisa, you're here to be light…"

_____

_____

_____

Pray, "Father, show me what You want me to learn in this passage." Now reread the verses and finish this sentence: God wants me to…

_____

_____

_____

My Prayer

_____

_____

_____

7

Make the Hour Count

Give your entire attention to what God is doing right now, and don't get worked up about what may or may not happen tomorrow. God will help you deal with whatever hard things come up when the time comes.

MATTHEW 6:34

Right now I don't want to miss anything. I want to make every day count. I want to cherish the hours and be aware of all the God-moments that happen all around me, not spend my days worrying about things I cannot control. I want to live a passionate life, not just survive. I want to read good books that encourage me to live life and have faith to the fullest. I want to surround myself with people who challenge me and build me up, not tear me down. Life is busy and full, but I want the chance to stop, listen, pay attention to God whispering in my ear.

Things on My Mind

Concerns, to-do lists, grocery lists, whatever—get these things down here so you can concentrate for the next ten minutes.

As I get older, I want to not care what I wear or what others think. I want everyone to see a sparkle in my eye that makes them smile. I want to feel confident in who I am and encourage others to be all they were created to be too. I want to laugh on the hour. I want to share special moments with friends and family. I want to walk every day, taking deep breaths because it feels good, not because it's good for me. I want to taste, smell, hear, see—really see—everything around me. I want to learn so I can be wise.

And when I'm an old woman and no longer able to get around and build up others, I want memories that will fill my mind. I want to have such a good friend in Jesus that I will never feel lonely. I want to spend my days in companionship with Him, filling the silence with prayer and praise and awaiting the time when I will join Him in heaven and hear, "Well done, good and faithful servant."

Lord God, teach me, teach me, and teach me again how to make the hour count. Don't let me allow the minutes to slide into hours, the hours into days, the days into weeks…until months and even years go by and I'm not sure what I accomplished. Let me count the small victories—with child, spouse, friend, neighbor—as accomplishments. Let me be proud of big and small moments, in a throw-back-the-shoulders sort of way, every time I stop to count them. I know You count them all. Thank You, Lord Jesus. Thank You for making me aware of how my life counts. How the past, present, and future count. And You are my timekeeper. Amen.

What Is God Saying to Me in This?

_____

_____

_____

Making the Scripture Mine

Jesus was so good about getting to the foundation of things—and it comforts me in an odd sort of way that people of His time got confused and stressed and worried. (I thought it was just me and our era!) In Matthew 6, He tells His people not to worry about food, clothes, or their very lives but instead to pay attention to the promise of today rather than the concerns of tomorrow.

Read the passage again slowly, as if Jesus had just placed His hands on your shoulders and halted you in whatever frenzied task you were about, to make you stand still and listen to what He has to say. Feel His words reverberate through your mind and heart. How would you restate the passage in your own words, for your life at this moment?

_____

_____

_____

Pray, "Father, show me what You want me to learn in this passage." Now reread the verse and finish this sentence: God wants me to…

_____

_____

_____

My Prayer

_____

_____

_____

8

Do Your Homework

I've thrown in my lot with you, GOD, and
I'm not budging.
Examine me, GOD, from head to foot,
order your battery of tests.
Make sure I'm fit
inside and out
So I never lose
sight of your love,
But keep in step with you,
never missing a beat.

PSALM 26:1–3

> ### Things on My Mind
>
> Concerns, to-do lists, grocery lists, whatever—get these things down here so you can concentrate for the next ten minutes.

My seven-year-old, Emma, just brought home her January creative writing paper. Here's how it reads, without edit: "These are some of my resolutions for the new year. First be nice to others. Next run faster. Next talk less listen more. Next watch less TV and do homework. Finally get my homework done. These are the things that I will change in 2006."

Being Emma's mom, I smile when I read her resolutions. I hear these things said to her by me, her father, her teacher, her choir director, her basketball coach, and others. They are the mantra she hears day in, day out. She's the kid who's been moved to the front of the class so her teacher can make sure she's paying attention. Yeah, that one.

Concentrating and following directions do not come easily to my second daughter, and therefore homework is not at the top of her favorites list. She'd much rather talk than listen. And she'd much rather put off her homework in favor of more fun things that capture her attention, such as watching television or playing with friends or her Polly Pockets.

I was a firstborn, a girl who loved rules and drawing neatly between the lines. So we don't have that in common. Need for speed? That wasn't me. But learning to talk less, listen more? Yeah, I need to pay attention to that. And focusing on the task at hand rather than all the things that pull at my mind and heart? That's tough for me to do too.

These days my God is asking me to do my homework—my home being my heart, my mind, my soul. He's working on me, bugging me to focus on Him, listen to Him, follow His direction. To learn how to love Him, truly love Him—heart, mind, and soul. But I tend to be just like my daughter. I want to do what He says, to follow directions, and I head out intending to do so. But then I'm swayed, distracted.

So once again I find myself sighing in frustration over my lack of concentration. I resolve to do what I've been told—to dig deep, to correct things in my homework that need correction, to focus on what I've been told, and to place my feet on the path I've been told to follow. *Do your homework,* I hear God saying to me. *Get it done. You can do it. I know you can. In you, because of Me, there is an A+ student just waiting to come out.*

Father God, sometimes I am lazy and unwilling to do the work You've set before me. I get distracted, choosing TV over time with You. Forgive me. Lead me. Show me how to get my act together and my priorities straight. Work in my life, my heart, Jesus. Ever onward. Amen.

What Is God Saying to Me in This?

_____

_____

_____

Making the Scripture Mine

David ends Psalm 25 with a call to God to redeem Israel (a.k.a. "us") "from all [her] troubles" (NIV). While it may sound as if David is saying he's perfect, he's not. He's saying he has integrity; he's obedient, and he trusts his God. Can we say the same? Reread the passage slowly, as if you were making your case to God. Does anything give you pause? How would you paraphrase the message in your own words?

_____

_____

_____

Pray, "Father, show me what You want me to learn in this passage." Now reread Psalm 26:1–3 and finish this sentence: God wants me to...

_____

_____

_____

My Prayer

_____

_____

_____

9

Cut 'Em Off at the Pass, Lord

Dear friend, take my advice;
it will add years to your life.
I'm writing out clear directions to Wisdom Way,
I'm drawing a map to Righteous Road.
I don't want you ending up in blind alleys,
or wasting time making wrong turns.
Hold tight to good advice; don't
     relax your grip.
Guard it well—your life is at stake!
Don't take Wicked Bypass;
don't so much as set foot on that
     road.
Stay clear of it; give it a wide berth.
Make a detour and be on your way.
PROVERBS 4:10–15

Things on My Mind

Concerns, to-do lists, grocery lists, whatever—get these things down here so you can concentrate for the next ten minutes.

_____

_____

_____

Last month during a flash flood, two fourteen-year-old boys drowned in the culvert a few blocks from our home. In another state, a teen heaved a brick off a freeway bridge and killed a young mother of two.

These young people made choices in a matter of moments that had life-time consequences. Choices that impacted not only their lives but many others—family, friends. In our neighborhood, in neighborhoods across the country, people are mourning bad choices that led to tragic results.

Perhaps you can relate. Maybe you know someone in a similar situation right now. Maybe that someone is you. Or maybe you look back at your past and fear that your children will make poor choices just as you did. I know there are many choices in my life that I regret, choices so foolish they make me shake my head today. Choices that placed me and others in harm's way. Choices that took me away from Jesus instead of closer to Him. Choices that were clearly sin, nothing more. It is only because of grace that I sit here today, thinking about those choices, writing a devotional.

I have a friend who prayed her children would be caught early on when they were doing wrong. My own prayer is that my children will be filled with wisdom, caution, care. That even while they explore, discover freedom, and spread their wings, they will make the choices God wishes them to make.

I'm pretty sure God urged those boys to get out of the arroyo when the rain started falling, and they probably ignored the warning in their gut. Perhaps they were even drawn to the water, daring fate, testing manhood. He must have told that teenager above the freeway that it was dangerous, foolish, wrong to throw the brick. But he did it anyway.

At least that's how He speaks to me. And I ignore Him too. We think we know better or that it's just fear pulling us back. We choose what we want to do rather than what we know we should do. We give in to the draw of foolhardy temptation over wise choices.

Learning to listen to God is a lifetime process. May our children learn to hear how He guides them earlier than we did!

God of Wisdom, I am afraid. I mourn for these families who are mourning choices made by foolish children. I fear that my own children will make a split-second decision that will affect the rest of their lives. Give them pause, Lord. Stop them in their tracks. Cut them off from paths of danger; make them wise beyond their years. Give them courage to follow Your wisdom, and help me teach them to read the danger signs. And help me do the same. Amen.

What Is God Saying to Me in This?

_____

_____

_____

Making the Scripture Mine

To me, the book of Proverbs often reads like one long advice column. So it's tempting to gloss over the wisdom passed down to us through the ages. But check out that first sentence again: if we listen, "it will add years" to our lives! This passage echoes other verses that say the fear of the Lord "will bring health to your body" (Proverbs 3:8, NIV) and "adds length to life" (Proverbs 10:27, NIV; see also Proverbs 9:10–11). It also echoes the famous story of King Solomon, who prayed for wisdom and who received God's promise of riches as well as long life if he obeyed God's commands (1 Kings 3:13–14).

Read Proverbs 4:10–15 again slowly, as if a wise old woman were pulling you aside and telling you a great secret. What's the core message for you, right now?

_____

_____

_____

Pray, "Father, show me what You want me to learn in this passage." Now reread the verses and finish this sentence: God wants me to...

_____

_____

_____

My Prayer

_____

_____

_____

_____

_____

_____

10

God Interruptions

I call Heaven and Earth to witness against you today: I place before you Life and Death, Blessing and Curse. Choose life so that you and your children will live. And love GOD, your God, listening obediently to him, firmly embracing him. Oh yes, he is life itself, a long life settled on the soil that GOD, your God, promised to give your ancestors, Abraham, Isaac, and Jacob.

DEUTERONOMY 30:19–20

I just learned that in the New Testament Greek, *bless* as in "God bless you" means "interrupt." So saying "God bless you" actually would've meant "May God interrupt your life."

I love this! All along I've thought of the phrase as a soother, something you say after someone sneezes or when someone heads out on a journey. I love the idea of telling someone, "God bless you," and knowing that I'm actually wishing that person a little bump up against the Holy One or perhaps a headlong slam right into the Creator of all.

What if we paid more attention to those times God blesses us with

Things on My Mind

Concerns, to-do lists, grocery lists, whatever—get these things down here so you can concentrate for the next ten minutes.

_____

_____

_____

interruptions? How often do we see challenges, obstacles, difficulties, traumas as little darts (or big spears) from the Evil One instead of as sweet hand-offs from the Lord on high? It's the old glass-half-full-or-half-empty question. How do we look at things? Can we change our perspective and therefore find joy in everything?

If we finish the phrase "May God bless you" with "and keep you," as some of us hear every Sunday at the end of our worship service, it gets even better. God wants to interrupt our lives, challenge us, make us aware that He was and is and is to come…but He doesn't want to send us away during those interrupting times. He wants to hold us tenderly in His arms, keep us the way a shepherd guards his sheep—caring, loving, protecting… He wants us to know Him better because of the interruption and therefore look forward to the next time we interface with Him in such a physical, distinct way.

So, dear friend, may God interrupt your life! May He stop you in the midst of your blurry, chaotic schedule; may He make you stay in bed for a day; may He make you look, really look, at your loved ones and know that each one is a gift from Him. And may you see any interruption as a divine invitation, to see and learn what He wants to teach you, even as He keeps you close.

Teach me, Lord Jesus, in everything, even those things I see as interruptions, inconveniences, irritations. Bless me in this way, Father, and help me see the blessing in all. Make me stop and wonder at the miracle of how You work in my life every day. Amen!

What Is God Saying to Me in This?

_____

_____

_____

Making the Scripture Mine

We don't usually turn to Deuteronomy when we're seeking spiritual insight. But while the name of the book means "repetition of the law," the main theme is the love relationship between the Lord and His people. Deuteronomy calls to us to be totally committed to the Lord in worship and obedience.

Deuteronomy 30:19–20 has fabulous depth and meaning. My *NIV Study Bible* notes say this in regard to "the LORD is your life": "The law, the Lord and life are bound together. 'Life' in this context refers to all that makes life rich, full and productive—as God created it to be."[2]

Read the passage again slowly, as if you were sitting at Moses' feet and he were speaking just to you. How would you reword the passage to speak directly to you today?

_____

_____

_____

Pray, "Father, show me what You want me to learn in this passage." Now reread the verses and finish this sentence: God wants me to...

_____

_____

_____

My Prayer

_____

_____

_____

Once You Learn, You Never Forget

I am GOD, the God of Abraham your father and the God of Isaac.
I'm giving the ground on which you are sleeping to you and to
your descendants.... All the families of the Earth will bless themselves in you and your descendants. Yes. I'll stay with you, I'll
protect you wherever you go, and I'll bring you back to this very
ground. I'll stick with you until I've done everything I promised
you.

GENESIS 28:13–15

I live on a suburban street where
young children are learning to ride
bicycles and older children are learning
to drive cars. The other day I decided
that my middle child, Emma, had
become embarrassingly old (almost
seven!) without knowing how to ride a
bike (what will the neighbors think?),
that it was some failure on my part as a
mother that I hadn't committed the
time and sweat equity to help her learn
(okay, sometimes guilt is justified). So
we went to the park.

Things on My Mind

Concerns, to-do lists, grocery
lists, whatever—get these
things down here so you can
concentrate for the next ten
minutes.

_____

_____

_____

My husband went with me to alternate on laps around the giant park with its winding sidewalk. He did a few turns, but Emma mostly wanted her mama with her. You've been there if you're a parent who has coached your child. *Can you feel that balance? Don't worry. I won't let go yet. Keep pedaling! Trust me. You're okay…you can do it. Say to yourself, Emma, "I can do it, I can do it, I can do it, I can do it…" Woohoo! You're doing it!!!*

Uh-oh! Look, you're okay! You can survive. Let's brush you off. No blood. You're okay. Hop back on that seat, and I'll get you going again. Wasn't that cool? I'm so proud of you! You can do it. I'm right here with you. I am so impressed. Keep after it. Start talking to yourself again, Emma. Say, "I can do it…" Keep pedaling. Feel that balance. Way to go! There you go!

Emma learned to ride a bike that day, and we clapped and celebrated and came home all smiles. I breathed a sigh of relief that my ongoing embarrassment as a failed mother was over. But what impressed me was not my own accomplishment; it was Emma. An hour later I peeked outside, and the girl was going around our cul-de-sac as if she had been biking for a year. It was as though she'd had this talent hidden just beneath the surface, begging to be released. She biked for hours that day, learning to handle curves and curbs, to go slow, to brake.

We're getting her a new twenty-inch bike for her birthday, complete with garish, girly markings and flashy ribbon streamers coming from the handlebars. She'll eat it up! And I've been thinking that I didn't really teach Emma to ride. Instead, she reminded me how God has put gifts and abilities within us and will help us use them if we're willing to try, to learn, to persist.

Again and again my Lord has to remind me to say to myself, *I can do it.* He has to remind me that He's right there beside me, holding me when I need help, releasing me when I don't. Following me. Cheering me on. Helping me get back up when I fall. Brushing me off. Getting me going again.

And then I ride. Remembering the balance. Sometimes even daring to take my hands off the handlebars. Wind rushing past me. Speed. Exhilaration. Freedom. Joy...

Lord God, I'm sorry that I give in to all the voices that call to me—other than Yours. I'm sorry that I worry about what others think and not only about what You think. Forgive me. Help me to find that balance again. Help me to find freedom and joy in what You've already taught me. Help me to become all You've created me to be. Thanks for never leaving me, always teaching me, and sometimes using my child to do both. Amen.

What Is God Saying to Me in This?

_____

_____

_____

Making the Scripture Mine

Sometimes I find it hard to believe that the God of my ancestors would take the time to pay attention to me. I mean, with billions of people in the world, doesn't He have more than enough to care for? Does He really care if I can ride a bike? Does He really care about my contribution? But obviously He does. One turn through Scripture, and I can see it a thousand times over—this love affair my God has with little ol' me.

Read Genesis 28:13–15 again slowly, as if God were speaking directly to you. How would you word the scripture for your circumstances today?

_____

_____

_____

_____

Pray, "Father, show me what You want me to learn in this passage." Now reread the verses and finish this sentence: God wants me to…

_____

_____

_____

My Prayer

_____

_____

Winter Weeding

Study this story of the farmer planting seed. When anyone hears news of the kingdom and doesn't take it in, it just remains on the surface, and so the Evil One comes along and plucks it right out of that person's heart. This is the seed the farmer scatters on the road.

The seed cast in the gravel—this is the person who hears and instantly responds with enthusiasm. But there is no soil of character, and so when the emotions wear off and some difficulty arrives, there is nothing to show for it.

The seed cast in the weeds is the person who hears the kingdom news, but weeds of worry and illusions about getting more and wanting everything under the sun strangle what was heard, and nothing comes of it.

The seed cast on good earth is the person who hears and takes in the News, and then produces a harvest beyond his wildest dreams.

MATTHEW 13:18–23

Things on My Mind

Concerns, to-do lists, grocery lists, whatever—get these things down here so you can concentrate for the next ten minutes.

_____

_____

_____

I just returned from a church service during which my dear friend Missie read these verses and spoke of how we have to examine our soil not just once in our lives, once a year, or once a month. We have to do it every day.

Now this idea makes me squirm in my seat a bit, because as much as I'd like to claim to be full of the Good Earth today or even to have the drama of the Gravel, I'm afraid I have to claim the Weedy Soil more often than not. I have some good stuff in my spiritual garden: excellent vegetation over here in the prayer section, fine compost over here in the confession corner, lovely bushes over here in the works section, promising sprouts over here… But throughout the garden are weeds—sprouting up among my straight rows of good growth, running amuck over there, virtually taking over the far corner.

What are the weeds in your spiritual life? In mine, there are the wild mustard seeds of envy, the thorns of jealousy, and the dirty, prickly, impossible-to-get-rid-of-forever thistles of pride. And there's prairie grass growing in the sandpit—of all places—evidence of sowing in places I wasn't ever meant to be. I like to act as if I'm Head Gardener when instead I should stick to my assigned tasks!

What are your weeds? I know they're there. I don't have any neighbors on my little suburban street who can claim a totally weed-free yard. If they have one glorious day in which they can shout, "I'm free! I'm weed free!" it is guaranteed to be short-lived. They cannot let their guard down, because every sunrise is likely to illuminate a new sprout. What's more, a neighbor's weed often spreads to our own yards, so we not only have to watch out for our own garden thistles, but we have to watch out for theirs too! It's a never-ending task, this weeding. Even in winter.

So as I stare out my window into a sleeting Colorado night, I figure I have some weeding to do. It's time to dig in again, to make sure I'm taking out what I know doesn't belong, fighting the good fight, using the right weed-killer—the Word of God. And I'll pry at those roots, clip down the stalks, rip out the leaves that try to claim my Good Earth and to steal the Light. Because I want my good growth to continue. I want to be a veritable Garden of Eden when Jesus comes again.

Hang on, Lord. I'm grabbing my trowel and my rake and my hoe. Show me where my weeds are. Forgive me for letting them get so out of control. Cleanse me, Father. Help me clean up my garden once more and make more room in my soil for You. Make me Good Earth. Thank You, Lord, for always being willing to put on Your sun hat and join me in the task. Thank You for the weeding You've already done in my life and all You will yet do. In Jesus' name. Amen.

What Is God Saying to Me in This?

_____

_____

_____

Making the Scripture Mine

Okay, so Jesus rarely interpreted His parables, but this one was important enough that He felt He had to spell it out for us. I like that about Him: on the most important stuff, He made it as simple and clear as possible.

Read Matthew 13:18–23 again slowly, as if you were sitting at Jesus' feet, listening first to the story, then His interpretation. How would you reword the scripture for your life?

_____

_____

_____

Pray, "Father, show me what You want me to learn in this passage." Now reread the verses and finish this sentence: God wants me to...

_____

_____

_____

My Prayer

_____

_____

_____

_____

_____

_____

13

Praying for Sexy

May God himself, the God who makes everything holy and whole, make you holy and whole, put you together—spirit, soul, and body—and keep you fit for the coming of our Master, Jesus Christ. The One who called you is completely dependable. If he said it, he'll do it!

1 THESSALONIANS 5:23–24

Coming up on fifteen years of marriage, I confess that sex is getting, um, rather rote. We shake it up on occasion, and my new Jazzercise routine is doing wonders for how I feel about myself (and Tim says that he appreciates the clingy Jazzercise wear).

With the changes in our bodies, three children roaming the house, day-to-day distractions, television, the end of baby making, financial stress, work stress, life/schedule stress...sex tends to take a backseat.

Things on My Mind

Concerns, to-do lists, grocery lists, whatever—get these things down here so you can concentrate for the next ten minutes.

_____

_____

_____

But God cautions us not to ignore this aspect of marital love. Every time Tim and I make love, I'm so grateful that we've made the time, found the energy. It renews our sense of closeness, of intimacy, and reminds us of an aspect of our love that we tend to forget for days on end. I get frustrated that it seems to be one more thing for my lists, as though I can write it out as a to-do item along with "shop for new shoes" or "pick up the dry cleaning." This is love! This is passion! Right?

I believe God can answer the most intimate of our heart cries. I know that He holds my best friend close as she mourns a tragedy and that He can ignite my desire for my husband and his desire for me. Bible teacher Beth Moore writes of a friend who prayed about her husband: "Every day I ask God that I might thrill to his touch."

Thrill to his touch? That sounds mighty good to me. There's no aspect of my life that my Savior is not interested in—including keeping my love life lively. He can help me remember the days I thrilled to Tim's touch, and he to mine.

So I am working on feeling better about myself, managing the stress through exercise, and reaching for my husband as often as possible. I provide him clues that I'm ready, I'm available. I retire to bed before I'm utterly exhausted and pray that God will remind me why I'm beautiful, desirable, sexy.

Satan will use any angle he can to undermine our marriages. Let's not let him divide us from our spouses on this front. Pray for sexy; pray for communication; pray for intimacy; pray for peace. Whatever you need, let God in, and He will help you on every front.

Creator, You obviously intend for me to desire my husband. Making love can be so much more than what we make it… Help us celebrate how You made us, and ignite a passion between us so we might celebrate it in the marriage bed. Strengthen our marriage on all fronts, and make our sex life the icing on the cake. Amen!

What Is God Saying to Me in This?

_____

_____

_____

Making the Scripture Mine

Even after much persecution and trauma in his life, Paul sounds utterly confident in the nature of God. The apostle's words reverberate with the theme: *God can do what He says He can do. He'll finish what He began.* The passage relates to my thoughts on sex in this way—that God began my love affair with Tim, and He'll see it through to the end. If I allow Him in and turn this aspect of my life over to Him as well, He'll make our sex life better than ever! This is a fairly liberal interpretation/application of the scripture, but I know God celebrates marital love and fidelity and wants us to find full satisfaction on this front as well.

Read 1 Thessalonians 5:23–24 again slowly, with hope and reverence. How would you word the scripture for your circumstances today?

_____

_____

_____

Pray, "Father, show me what You want me to learn in this passage." Now reread the verses and finish this sentence: God wants me to...

_____

_____

_____

My Prayer

_____

_____

14

Saying Hi to Stormie

> This is how much God loved the world: He gave his Son, his one
> and only Son. And this is why: so that no one need be destroyed;
> by believing in him, anyone can have a whole and lasting life.
>
> JOHN 3:16

Stormie Omartian is sitting on my plane. I spotted her
before I got on, standing by the
wall with the other first classers, fan-
ning herself. She was on before zone
one was even called, meaning she must
be a Million Miler or whatever that air-
line calls their most frequent fliers.

In case you don't know her, she has
sales that approach Lucado's and Dob-
son's. She's the author of *The Power of
a Praying Wife* (and …*of a Praying Parent* and …*of a Praying Husband*, etc.),
the series you see every time you go to
a Wal-Mart or a Christian bookstore.
I've not read all her books, but I look
up to her, like a new Brownie to a
Junior Girl Scout. She has gone before me. She has inspired people like
Beth Moore, another woman who makes me behave like a silly teenager
with an idol. Stormie doesn't look old enough for the title, but I feel as

Things on My Mind

Concerns, to-do lists, grocery
lists, whatever—get these
things down here so you can
concentrate for the next ten
minutes.

_____
_____
_____
_____

though she's the grandmother of female Christian writers. Maybe she can help me... How? I don't know.

I rehearse my introduction silently. "Hi, Stormie. I'm Lisa Bergren. I'm a Christian writer too."

Nah. Too lame. Writer of what? But too much more is too...out there.

"Excuse me. Are you Stormie Omartian?"

Still lame. I know who she is. It's like lying.

"Stormie, thank you for all you've done for the kingdom."

Blech. Too churchy.

"Hi, I just wanted to say hello. I'm a Christian writer too..."

Maybe. Assumes nothing. Friendly without being in her face. I'll just be passing by her in the aisle anyway. There won't be time for any real conversation.

I wait until the first five zones are called and then board with the rush of zone sixers, all of us apparently in a mad dash to stand in the hot Jetway. Slowly we trickle in, and I spot her in row two, laughing with a girl I assume is her daughter. They're still laughing and whispering together as I edge by, so I hold back, waiting until they look up. But they don't. And I don't say a word.

I step forward to row three, feeling my cowardice. When I reach my seat, 9E, I sit down and stare out the window. It's only as the plane begins to roll forward, steadily gaining speed, and I say my customary prayer of protection for the plane and our crew and all of us inside that the thought hits me. *If Stormie is on this plane, there's no way God is calling us home yet. We're safer with her aboard. Think of all the work she has left to do! God wouldn't waste that opportunity...*

My eyes pop open in surprise. *What?*

Why do I think God would save our plane from a fiery wreck because a world-famous writer is aboard? Where did this radical sense of insufficiency, inadequacy come from? Why am I afraid to introduce myself to her?

Who's to say I don't have as much to accomplish for God as she does? Or maybe the guy beside me? (Okay, not him; he's hogging the whole armrest.) Or the grandma ten rows back or the kid bouncing in front of me?

I've been blessed with great opportunities and some successes, but feelings of inadequacy have never left me. I'm guessing even Stormie feels inadequate at times. I never even gave her a chance before I popped her up on that Pedestal of Perfection and walked away. But the goal is for all of us to see ourselves as Jesus sees us: perfectly created, perfectly forgiven, perfectly worthy, perfectly loved, perfectly covered by His grace alone.

I settle back in my seat and think that next time I'll smile and stick out my hand and shake hers and say, "Hi, Stormie." Even if that's *all* I say.

Savior, when will I feel the full value of Your love? When will these nagging feelings of inadequacy leave me and only the confidence of Your love remain within me? Why do I strive for success rather than desire simply to serve? Father, continue to do Your good work within me, teaching me, molding me into one of Your worthy ones. Amen.

What Is God Saying to Me in This?

_____

_____

_____

Making the Scripture Mine

It's the verse you see on bracelets and banners, the most famous and most frequently memorized verse in the Bible. It's the verse that should be that central and easily rattled off, because it contains the core of the gospel: God's love, God's sacrifice, God's saving story, God's accessibility.

Read John 3:16 again slowly, as if you were listening to a man you love say these words to you, with tears streaming down his face, his eyes awash in the urgency that you understand and absorb each syllable. How would you reword the passage for your circumstances today?

_____

_____

_____

Pray, "Father, show me what You want me to learn in this passage." Now reread the verse and finish this sentence: God wants me to…

_____

_____

_____

My Prayer

_____

_____

_____

Part 2

Spring

Twenty-Twenty Perspective

Doom to you! You pretend to have the inside track.
You shut GOD out and work behind the scenes,
Plotting the future as if you knew everything....
You have everything backwards!
You treat the potter as a lump of clay.
Does a book say to its author,
"He didn't write a word of me"?
Does a meal say to the woman who cooked it,
"She had nothing to do with this"?...
"In holy worship they'll honor the Holy One of Jacob
and stand in holy awe of the God
    of Israel.
Those who got off-track will get
    back on-track,
and complainers and whiners learn
    gratitude."

ISAIAH 29:15–16, 23–24

This past week I obsessed over my typical daily life—writing deadline, my fifth grader's stressed-out view of the world ("Mama, my life is so hard!"), finances, work responsibilities, juggling the family schedule...and

Things on My Mind

Concerns, to-do lists, grocery lists, whatever—get these things down here so you can concentrate for the next ten minutes.

then I watched news program after news program of Hurricane Katrina's impact on the city of New Orleans and beyond.

At times my vision of my world needs a good prescription lens. Sometimes all I can think about is the future—what will come, when it will come. Once in a while all I can think about is the past—what has happened, why it happened. Seldom do I stay immersed in the present, enjoying what is, not worrying about what was or what is to come.

My *Time* magazine arrived today, the cover a haunting photo of a black woman, perhaps about my age, her severely injured mother in her arms, surrounded by water. She is looking about in desperation, in grief, crying, shouting. Again, like that first night I could not stop watching MSNBC, CNN, FOX—constantly rotating between the three as if the next channel would surely show something better, something hopeful—and I am brought up short.

I have no legitimate crisis in my life. My family is healthy. We have a home. Two cars. Clothing. A great church. Work. People who are frantic and lost and searching—for a new place to live, for a place to work, for missing loved ones—this is legitimate crisis.

Why can't I live in the present? Why can't I enjoy what is, today? I long to take what is right in my life every day and build upon that, but it is difficult. Instead I am distracted, constantly needing that special perspective lens.

Disaster could be around the corner for any of us. But we cannot live in fear of what might be, only in praise for what is right now. Appreciation, celebration. Every day is a miracle. There is always something good, something right, we can focus on, beginning with our faith in the Savior who sees all—and all perfectly.

Father God, please help me see things with Your twenty-twenty perspective. Forgive me for languishing behind what You're trying to teach me today; forgive me for leaping ahead, constantly trying to plan my life instead of waiting on You. Give me Your perspective, Lord, and Your peace and pleasure in today. And please, please be with all the people who truly are in crisis today, calling for You. Amen.

What Is God Saying to Me in This?

_____

_____

_____

Making the Scripture Mine

I love the book of Isaiah; it's a book I often turn to when I need a passage to reassure me, lift me up, or screw my head back on straight. *Isaiah* means "the Lord saves," which I find perfect, because his writings remind me constantly of that. Here Isaiah is hitting his stride—stern and fearsome in his dire warnings, hopeful and light in his promises.

Read the Isaiah 29 passage again slowly, as if Isaiah were writing to you alone. How would you reword the passage for your circumstances today?

_____

_____

_____

Pray, "Father, show me what You want me to learn in this passage." Now reread the verses and finish this sentence: God wants me to...

_____

_____

_____

_____

My Prayer

_____

_____

_____

_____

_____

_____

16

Bottle-Fed Babes Forever

So clean house! Make a clean sweep of malice and pretense, envy and hurtful talk. You've had a taste of God. Now, like infants at the breast, drink deep of God's pure kindness. Then you'll grow up mature and whole in God.

1 PETER 2:1–3

When my youngest, Jack, had long since been weaned from the breast and had officially outgrown bottles, his father lobbied for the leap to sippy cups. The pediatrician specifically told us to "quit the bottle." But still…I hesitated. I hesitated to allow Jack that step, feeling as if I were handing him the keys to the car and saying, "Don't be out too late, mister." You gotta understand—he's my youngest. He's my baby. After him, there are no more bottles.

So I ran the dishwasher one more time and mournfully set the nipples in

Things on My Mind

Concerns, to-do lists, grocery lists, whatever—get these things down here so you can concentrate for the next ten minutes.

_____

_____

_____

neat stacks and the bottles in perfect rows on the shelves, even though I knew Jack would never suck from them again. But I wasn't ready to toss them. I needed them here, near me. I'd part from them when I was good and ready.

What was that all about? Like so many times in parenting, it isn't the child who has a hard time with a transition; it's the parent. Jack was clearly ready. When I put him down one night, he said halfheartedly, "Mi-ilk." But when I said, "No, no, sweet pea; just water if you're thirsty," he rolled over and accepted it. Then he promptly went to sleep.

What was it within me that wanted him to cry? to demand that I give him a bottle, demand that I give him his nightly milk? Heaven knows, we'd seen his sisters put up a fuss. But not this child. He's compliant. A prince. Just when I didn't want an easy baby.

I think what I was feeling is that mother-babe connection. Jack's independence from a bottle was one more step away from the breast, from me. I was mourning his independence, wanting to draw him closer and hold him for a moment longer before he became a quarterback or a lawyer or a father himself. Suddenly it seemed my days as a mom were numbered. I was heading into a new era. A brave new world.

Perhaps this is what God feels: wanting to celebrate each of our steps, while longing to cradle us close. Urging us along—*you can do it*—but aching to keep one hand on our shoulder, keep us safe, while we try our shaky legs. How to learn from Him to allow space and yet be near? to encourage and yet not smother? to foster freedom that, in turn, fosters a desire to return? I have much yet to learn from the Master.

Papa God, thank You for weaning me from my own bottle. Thank You for staying near and yet always encouraging me onward. Thank You for always asking me to take the next step, and then the next, never satisfied to let me languish. Help me have the same courage with my children. Give me insight and vision for the future, joy in the prospect of all they could be in maturity, and help me not dwell in what has been and mourn what can no longer be. May I greet every day with joy, Jesus. I thank You for my life and for my children! Amen.

What Is God Saying to Me in This?

_____

_____

_____

Making the Scripture Mine

My *NIV Study Bible* says this of 1 Peter 2:2: "The unrestrained hunger
of a healthy baby provides an example of the kind of eager desire for spiritual food that ought to mark the believer. 'Spiritual milk' probably
[refers] to God's word."[3]

Read the passage again slowly, as if you were picking up the second
page of a letter written only for you by the apostle Peter. How would you
paraphrase the scripture for your circumstances today?

_____

_____

_____

Pray, "Father, show me what You want me to learn in this passage." Now
reread the verses and finish this sentence: God wants me to…

_____

_____

_____

My Prayer

_____

_____

_____

17

Go Fish

Turn your back on sin; do something good.
Embrace peace—don't let it get away!
GOD keeps an eye on his friends,
his ears pick up every moan and groan.
GOD won't put up with rebels;
he'll cull them from the pack.
Is anyone crying for help? GOD is listening,
ready to rescue you.
If your heart is broken, you'll find
    GOD right there;
if you're kicked in the gut, he'll
        help you catch your breath.
Disciples so often get into trouble;
still, GOD is there every time.
                PSALM 34:14–19

Things on My Mind

Concerns, to-do lists, grocery lists, whatever—get these things down here so you can concentrate for the next ten minutes.

_____

_____

_____

M y second grader grappled with an injustice last week. We pull her out of school fifteen minutes early on Wednesdays in order to get to piano and church on the same night. Apparently, on a Wednesday the music teacher handed out roles for the second-grade play, *Go Fish,* and since Emma wasn't there, she was the only one not to get a specific role or a unique costume.

Now this seemed unfair to me, but I didn't know if it was the whole story, so I stayed out of it and tried to coach Emma into thinking it was nice to avoid the pressure to remember extra songs, lines, etc. But still she longed for the coveted sea-horse role—or even a clown fish or electric eel. The night before the performance she was in tears, clearly upset about the fact that *everyone* was *something* except her.

I felt bad for Emma, but this was the night before the play, and I didn't want to be Commando Mom, going in and demanding a role for her starlet-in-waiting. So again I comforted the child while thinking evil thoughts about the music teacher.

Since Tim couldn't attend the evening show for parents, he went to the afternoon performance for the school and came home a bit chagrined. Emma had been right—she was the only one without a role. Every other child was part of a sea-horse or electric-eel or clown-fish group or had individual speaking roles. It was as though she had been cut right out!

Inside I seethed. On the way to the show, her older sister, Olivia, said something about how unfair it was. (She'd seen the afternoon show too.) I immediately said something nasty and sarcastic like, "Yeah, it really makes sense that the *music* teacher cuts Emma out of a role because she had to go to *piano*." We talked about how she probably had made a rash decision and then stubbornly held on to save face.

We settled into folding chairs toward the back, and Jack stood on my lap to see. Then right before it started, up popped Emma beside us, her face splitting into a huge grin. "I'm a sea horse! I'm a sea horse! She says I can be a sea horse too!"

I grinned back at her, so glad the teacher had finally seen the light. The play progressed, as second-grade plays do, with kids shouting or whispering lines, taking tons of time to adjust microphones *just right* before speaking, losing their hats, forgetting their lines...and Emma proudly joined the sea horses and sang all the songs, her pride restored.

Afterward I thought about how I could've handled the situation better. I could've investigated a bit more when Emma first told me she had no role in the play (without assuming she was exaggerating or assuming the worst of the teacher). And I could've trusted God to make it all right somehow and focused on His wheels of justice and His ultimate plan for Emma rather than my own dark thoughts. He could've made a no-role situation work out as well as he had the sea-horse scenario.

So I confessed to my kids that I had blown it, and I confessed to God too. I wanted them to see that sometimes we adults behave in ways that we need to change.

Life is full of Go Fish moments when you don't know what card you'll pull. Sometimes it's the right one; sometimes it's the worst one. But whatever card it is, God remains Lord over all and will see to our ultimate well-being. And He'll do that for our kids too.

Father God, I'm sorry that I am so overly concerned about justice in my world—justice the way I see it rather than the way You see it. I promise to try to trust You more and more each day with the things that impact us. I see You working. I know You are here with us. Thank You for that. I pray that You will always remain close to us, Your stubborn and willful children. In Jesus' name. Amen.

What Is God Saying to Me in This?

_____

_____

_____

Making the Scripture Mine

My *NIV Study Bible* says this of Psalm 34:15–18: "Assurance that the Lord hears the prayers of the righteous. He so thoroughly thwarts those who do evil that they are forgotten."[4] These verses are satisfying and affirming!

Read the passage again slowly, this time as if it were a personal statement of faith. (For example: *I will turn my back from sin; I will embrace peace... God has His eye on me!*)

Sometimes personalizing scripture like that helps me to understand it better, to absorb it. How would you word the key phrases of the scripture for your life today?

_____

_____

_____

Pray, "Father, show me what You want me to learn in this passage." Now reread the verses and finish this sentence: God wants me to...

_____

_____

_____

My Prayer

_____

_____

_____

18

Heaven's Bread of Life

During the meal, Jesus took and blessed the bread, broke it, and
gave it to his disciples:
"Take, eat.
This is my body."
Taking the cup and thanking God, he gave it to them:
"Drink this, all of you.
This is my blood,
God's new covenant poured out for
     many people
for the forgiveness of sins.
I'll not be drinking wine from this
cup again until that new day when
I'll drink with you in the kingdom
of my Father."
                    MATTHEW 26:26–29

> ### Things on My Mind
>
> Concerns, to-do lists, grocery
> lists, whatever—get these
> things down here so you can
> concentrate for the next ten
> minutes.
>
> _____
>
> _____
>
> _____

I t is Holy Week—the week we remember Jesus' last days on Earth. I
took Olivia to a drama presentation at
church tonight. There we walked from
one station to another in small groups, witnessing scenes from Jesus' life,
from birth to death. It was powerful and intimate and moving and, at
times, surprising. I never get over the shock and sorrow that He had to
die—for me—so that I might live.

As we drove home, we talked about how Jesus loves Olivia so much that He would've come for her even if she were the only one on Earth.

"The *only* one?" she repeated.

"The only one," I said. "He loves you that much. He loves *me* that much. That's the amazing kind of God we serve. Even when we run away—like that disciple at the end who denied Him—even then He loves us enough to die for us."

We talked about how our lives are a drop in the bucket but heaven will be like a waterfall of time. Forever. Eternity. Days upon days to do nothing but worship our God and serve Him as He ought to have been served on Earth. How we should do all we can to serve Him now, even if it comes at a price…

Two years ago my six-year-old niece died. At her memorial service, they served communion, and when we were walking up, tears streaming down our faces, Olivia asked if she could take it.

I told the pastor that this was Mady's cousin and that she'd like to take her first communion, if that was all right. He smiled and hunched down, looking her in the eye. Holding a piece of bread up to her, he said, "This is the same bread that Mady is eating in heaven *right now.* The same bread that you will eat when you are together again."

It makes me smile to think of Madison up there, eating away, celebrating. It makes her seem closer to me when I take communion and remember that through Jesus, we are one. We are one body in the Christ who loves us *each* so much that He would die for us *right now.* Nothing on Earth compares to what is ahead. And when we eat the bread and drink the wine, may we understand that God wants nothing more than to live in us, shine through us, breathe through us, cleanse us, keep us, sustain us, love us. He wants to be our main sustenance. He is everything we really need. Forever.

Father God, thank You for sending Your Son for me. Please, Lord, cleanse me; forgive me for all the ways I fall short and sin against You. Thank

You, Father, for loving me beyond anything I've ever experienced. Thank You for dying so I might live. In Jesus' name. Amen.

What Is God Saying to Me in This?

_____

_____

_____

Making the Scripture Mine

The Eucharist makes some of us uncomfortable. The symbolism is so very...brutal, almost cannibalistic to eat bread as if it were Christ's body and drink wine as if it were His blood. But spend time in the Old Testament, and you'll more fully see the reason, the need, for such a total and complete sacrifice. We needed the new covenant. Only God could establish it, once and for all, with us. In Christ's blood, poured out for us, we are covered. Completely, from head to toe. Cleansed. Protected. Claimed.

Read Matthew 26:26–29 again slowly, as if you were sitting at a low table, watching Jesus lift the bread and break it, then lift the cup and stretch out His hands, offering it to you. How would you word the scripture as if He were speaking to you alone?

_____

_____

_____

Pray, "Father, show me what You want me to learn in this passage." Now reread the verses and finish this sentence: God wants me to...

_____

_____

_____

My Prayer

_____

_____

_____

_____

_____

19

Language Barriers

A green Shoot will sprout from Jesse's stump,
from his roots a budding Branch.
The life-giving Spirit of GOD will hover over him,
the Spirit that brings wisdom and understanding,
The Spirit that gives direction and builds strength,
the Spirit that instills knowledge and Fear-of-GOD....
The wolf will romp with the lamb....
The whole earth will be brimming with knowing God-Alive,
a living knowledge of God ocean-deep, ocean-wide.

ISAIAH 11:1–2, 6, 9

I've gone and done something crazy. I've hauled my eldest, Olivia, out of her last days of school and brought her with me to Venice on a research trip. She's beside herself with excitement, her eyes as wide as saucers as she takes in everything about her. We've rented an apartment in a family-oriented part of the city called Castello.

While I'm agog about the ancient culture, the living, breathing history all around us, she's more intrigued with the current culture, the way people gesture with their hands and congregate

Things on My Mind

Concerns, to-do lists, grocery lists, whatever—get these things down here so you can concentrate for the next ten minutes.

on the street each night to chat with their neighbors and make purchases one store or stall at a time rather than in a Wal-Mart Supercenter. The church bells ring loudly enough to wake us, and stray dogs seem to wander the same streets day after day, unclaimed yet somehow cared for by all.

On our first evening in Venice, we unpack and then head out to San Marco Square, where Olivia lays eyes on one of the most famed churches in the world, on one of the most famed piazzas in the world. We gaze at the lagoon, its green waves lapping at the bricks at our feet, and then head back toward our home away from home. We settle into chairs in a street-side trattoria with a view down the wide Calle Garibaldi to the ocean and St. Mary's across the water.

We eat, shamefully, from a menu marked *Tourista* because I'm too jet-lagged to consider anything else. *Spaguetti Bolognesa, insalata* (salad), and a lightly fried chicken breast—hardly adventurous Italian eating. Before we're done, Liv heads out to see two old well caps that are a hallmark of Venice—the locked-off ancient cisterns that once brought its citizens the only fresh water available. They are in every square we cross.

But it is two girls huddled together chatting that draws Olivia's attention. She returns to me, excitedly telling me they're her age and asking if she can speak to them. "Sure, sure," I say and watch as she tentatively approaches and begins speaking to them. The two girls huddle closer and laugh, gesticulating wildly, and then turn back to Olivia. The three of them begin ten feet apart, and in minutes they're three feet apart. My heart swells with pride. How brave my girl is! I love watching her reach out, trying to talk, smiling, halting, searching for words, but sticking with it.

I pay the bill and join them twenty minutes into their stilted conversation. They are trying to get different aspects of their lives across to one another, as excited about this connection as if they had met someone from another planet. After a time, we leave them and return to our apartment. I know Olivia will watch for the girls all week. Children hunger for other children. It's a need within her that she'll try to find a way to fulfill.

That leaves me thinking of communication itself tonight—that longing for connection. Why is it that when we have those "connecting moments" with God, we're left breathless and surprised? We know He's there as surely as we know there are neighbors next door. And yet when we reach out, risk a little, try to talk to Him, and He responds, we find ourselves surprised.

What would it take for us to welcome Him with joy rather than surprise? What kind of experience would it take to become so comfortable with our Savior that we expect Him to be there?

People talk about "when God shows up." God is always there. It's more like when *people* show up—when we tune in, try to bridge the gap between us, attempt to bridge the language barriers between the human and the holy.

The thing we have to keep remembering? God has already made the way. All we need to do is walk on it so often that the path becomes worn and our steps become sure. Then, then, we will stroll arm in arm with Him, listening, learning, loving, laughing.

> *Lord, I don't know why I constantly fall out of communication with You. Please forgive me. I write e-mails and talk on the phone every day, but one of the first things I let go of in my busy schedule is prayer. Forgive me. Cleanse me. Make me new. Renew my hunger to reach out to You, to feel You reaching out to me. Bust through our language barrier. Give me ears to hear and a tongue with words that You welcome. Hold me, Jesus. Hold me close. I want to feel Your heartbeat. I want to know You. Day in and day out, forever and ever. Amen.*

What Is God Saying to Me in This?

_____

_____

Making the Scripture Mine

These verses from Isaiah 11 are some of the most famous prophetic words spoken of the coming Messiah and the coming Messianic age (when Jesus returns). When you read the first half of Isaiah 11, you get a glimpse of heaven, a foreign world where little children lead lions about. (Am I the only one envisioning Aslan from Narnia?)

Read the passage again slowly, as if you were the first person to ever read these famous prophetic words. Picture them on old papyrus in a script you can barely decipher but hungrily scan, wanting to absorb every promising word. How would you paraphrase it for your life today?

_____

_____

_____

Pray, "Father, show me what You want me to learn in this passage." Now reread the verses and finish this sentence: God wants me to...

_____

_____

_____

My Prayer

_____

_____

_____

20

Ugly Americans

> [Jesus] went on to open their understanding of the Word of God, showing them how to read their Bibles this way. He said, "You can see now how it is written that the Messiah suffers, rises from the dead on the third day, and then a total life-change through the forgiveness of sins is proclaimed in his name to all nations— starting from here, from Jerusalem! You're the first to hear and see it. You're the witnesses."
>
> LUKE 24:45–48

Things on My Mind

Concerns, to-do lists, grocery lists, whatever—get these things down here so you can concentrate for the next ten minutes.

_____

_____

_____

Much of the world sees Americans as open-hearted and simple, loud and obnoxious, uncouth and disrespectful. We're the new kids on the block, having not earned our history yet. The nouveau riche, holding power but not having earned respect.

On the way to Italy, Liv and I were in the Frankfurt airport, trying to catch a couple of hours of sleep during a layover. We awakened to a man loudly speaking his mind on the war in Iraq: "foreigners who don't bathe" and the "need to wipe out a whole lot of them with a good old-fashioned bomb."

I cringed and rolled over, wishing he'd shut up, embarrassed by his manner, embarrassed to call him a fellow American.

The next day we were on a crowded water-bus, traveling the Grand Canal. Another American man, frustrated by his inability to get on because everyone was moving so slowly, shouted out, "Get the hell on the #*$&$*@ bus!" Again I cringed and felt ashamed of my fellow American.

Two days later we ran across a group of college kids, clearly drunk, stumbling down a local street, undoubtedly waking up others on a sleepy, neighborhood *calle.* Yet another instance of disrespectful Americans. I wished I could put duct tape over each of their mouths and send them back to their hotel.

I watch how people react to such Americans. The natives recoil, looking down on us as a people when individuals like these are our representatives. I want to prove them wrong about what they're thinking—by learning a bit of the language of the country I'm touring, by saying *per favore* and *grazie,* and by leaving very little garbage in my wake. I spend money and respect national treasures. I admire and appreciate everything around me. And yet I'm sure I've stepped on toes or made others wince at least once or twice.

My point is this: When am I an ugly American? Moreover, when am I an ugly Christian? When do I embarrass God and make Him wince? I want Him to glow with pride, point down at me, and whisper to Saint Pete, "That's my girl." I want to reflect His light, with peace and joy in my eyes, to all I meet.

Lord, I know that I must embarrass You sometimes. Please forgive me and help me be a better representative of You and Your light to the world. Keep me from stepping on toes; keep respect in my words and tone of voice; keep my actions to those that communicate welcome, peace, kindness. Help me stamp out the darkness within me. Draw others to You through me, in spite of me, Lord. Draw them. Amen.

What Is God Saying to Me in This?

_____

_____

_____

Making the Scripture Mine

Being a witness for Christ in the first century was vital. If it hadn't been for those early believers, how far would the gospel have spread? We've lost a sense of urgency for the task before us: the call to be messengers of light in a world of darkness. And yet it is as important as ever for us to take the call seriously, to be witnesses for Christ in everything we say and do.

Read Luke 24:45–48 again slowly, as if you were hearing the call of Christ for the first time. How would you paraphrase it for your life today?

_____

_____

_____

Pray, "Father, show me what You want me to learn in this passage." Now reread the verses and finish this sentence: God wants me to...

_____

_____

_____

My Prayer

_____

_____

_____

21

Swinging Midgets

The gossip of bad people gets them in trouble;
the conversation of good people keeps them out of it.
Well-spoken words bring satisfaction;
well-done work has its own reward.
Fools are headstrong and do what they like;
wise people take advice....
Rash language cuts and maims,
but there is healing in the words of the wise.
PROVERBS 12:13–15, 18

Things on My Mind

Concerns, to-do lists, grocery lists, whatever—get these things down here so you can concentrate for the next ten minutes.

_____
_____
_____

The waters that surround Venice and flow into the Adriatic Sea are a murky sea-foam green, pretty enough, but not nearly what they used to be. As recently as the '30s and '40s, the water was a crystalline turquoise. After World War II, all that changed. Deep channels were dug to reach a new oil refinery on the mainland. Other deep channels were dug between Venice and the outer Giudecca, allowing giant cruise ships to move through. The dredging and the resulting traffic keep the water in a constant state of moving silt, giving it a milky look.

Some of us have been so wounded in life that it's as if a giant trench has been cut into our torso, slicing heart and gut. The wounds heal after time, but the scars remain. And new wounds seem to travel familiar paths, making us wince at the familiarity of the pain.

I'm constantly amazed at how people allow others near—others who are cutting and negative or who routinely cause them harm. As Christians, we often allow such people close out of a sense of duty. But I maintain that we need to allow them near only if we sense God's call of compassion and are in such a place of strength that we can be a witness to them without being hurt by them. But few of us are that strong—like the cartoonish strong man who can keep the swinging midget away from his body with one arm on the midget's head.

All wounds take time to heal. It is possible for a channel to settle, for the water to become clear again. But sometimes we allow cruise ships and oil tankers to dredge up the silt in our channels over and over. Channels are a part of life, but we can stop the traffic, or we can redirect it. And we can allow the salt water to wash over our wounds and heal us. We can allow life to again flow over that segment of our souls so we can truly move on—changed and yet whole.

My wounded Christ, You knew such hurt...and total healing. You can understand my pain. Help me draw healthy boundaries so You can fully heal me. Take my life and show me where I need to say yes, where I need to say no. Show me how I should speak to others with peace and love and yet remain forthright and strong. I look to You, Lord. Amen.

What Is God Saying to Me in This?

_____

_____

_____

Making the Scripture Mine

Proverbs clearly delineates between wisdom and foolishness, good and evil. Over and over again we make choices, every day, every hour even, in how we are to live and how we allow others to affect us.

Read the passage again slowly, as if you were listening to a beloved teacher. How would you word the message for your life today?

_____

_____

_____

Pray, "Father, show me what You want me to learn in this passage." Now reread the verses and finish this sentence: God wants me to…

_____

_____

_____

My Prayer

_____

_____

_____

22

Venice Espionage

Real wisdom, God's wisdom, begins with a holy life and is characterized by getting along with others. It is gentle and reasonable, overflowing with mercy and blessings, not hot one day and cold the next, not two-faced. You can develop a healthy, robust community that lives right with God and enjoy its results *only* if you do the hard work of getting along with each other, treating each other with dignity and honor.

JAMES 3:17–18

I spy on them from our second-floor apartment.

I, a child of the American suburbs, am fascinated by this nightly Venetian ritual. From our window, I watch the evening meet-and-greet, and I come to understand that this is just part of the schedule Monday through Saturday. Across from me, newcomers from another neighborhood stream in under a sign that reads *Sotoportego e Calle Firziera.*

Things on My Mind

Concerns, to-do lists, grocery lists, whatever—get these things down here so you can concentrate for the next ten minutes.

_____

_____

_____

_____

A woman emerges from the bar across the street, all gray hair and support hose and geriatric shoes, with two glasses of the sweet *grappa* that Venetians favor in her hands. She settles at a table beside a gray-haired man in a gray jacket and blue socks, white calves showing, arms crossed, legs crossed, watching, watching. The man barely acknowledges the gift—is he husband, brother, neighbor, friend to the woman? His eyes follow a pair of young women in tight jeans stroll down the street, seeing them dimly, not really concentrating.

Two men draw closer, and the three males begin an animated conversation. Life enters the first man's eyes, and he smiles. One of the newcomers speaks to the old woman in support hose, and she nods and smiles. This is the routine: watching, gathering, talking, separating, gathering, watching, departing. Kids buzz by on Rollerblades, and the older generation watches them with a mix of consternation and wonder. Teenagers and college students pass by, occasionally waving and calling out a *Buona sera*, before moving on to full lives, active lives. They're too busy to stop.

But I am entranced by this older generation of Venetians, the ones who walk their grandchildren in strollers and allow their toddlers to suck on pacifiers way beyond their infant years and pause only to chat with those who waylay them to admire and coo at their grandbabies.

It is this generation of people over sixty that seems to be the keepers of this culture. And I long for something similar in my Colorado Springs neighborhood. I want a time when we all come out and talk, connect, share. I want older people who will come and admire my babies and give me advice on how to raise them. I want community.

This hunger is God given. Hillary Clinton did not come up with "It takes a village." God did. Without community, without fellowship, we cannot help one another along the path of faith. We cannot grow stronger, deeper, wider in our faith.

So I'll go to the next church mixer where I can get to know new people in the congregation. I'll take part in small-group and Bible-study opportunities. And maybe I'll even take cookies to my neighbors.

Father of us all, sometimes reaching out to my brothers and sisters—let alone to strangers on the street—seems more than I have energy for. Live in me; breathe in me. Make me courageous, outgoing. Help me take honest, God-given interest in every soul I meet. Work through us all to make us better than we are today. Use our community, Father, one neighbor at a time. Amen.

What Is God Saying to Me in This?

_____

_____

_____

Making the Scripture Mine

Living in peace with others is work—almost physical work. Christian righteousness comes from loving others, forgiving them, giving them the benefit of the doubt. Too often we judge or write someone off rather than give in to the call to love.

Read James 3:17–18 again slowly, as if you're gaining knowledge that will serve you for the rest of your life. How would you filter down the scripture for your life today?

_____

_____

_____

Pray, "Father, show me what You want me to learn in this passage." Now reread the verses and finish this sentence: God wants me to…

_____

_____

_____

My Prayer

_____

_____

_____

_____

_____

_____

23

Vulnerable in Venice

GOD met me more than halfway,
he freed me from my anxious fears.
Look at him; give him your warmest smile.
Never hide your feelings from him.
When I was desperate, I called out,
and GOD got me out of a tight spot.
GOD's angel sets up a circle
of protection around us while we pray.
Open your mouth and taste, open your eyes and see—
how good GOD is.
Blessed are you who run to him.

PSALM 34:4–8

Things on My Mind

Concerns, to-do lists, grocery lists, whatever—get these things down here so you can concentrate for the next ten minutes.

_____

_____

_____

Here in Venice with my daughter, I'm feeling more vulnerable than I've ever felt before. The man at the grocery store makes fun of me as I fumble through an order at the deli counter, and I can't even make out which cutting words he uses as he makes his co-worker giggle and cast sideways glances our way. The man in the fish market offers us raw shrimp, one for Olivia and one for me. Not that we'd usually eat raw shrimp in an open-air market (seems rather unwise), but I'm torn between doing it for acceptance by this fish salesman and wondering if he's yet another person laughing at our expense. I toss them back to him. *You do it,* I intone play-fully, using a look and gesture that cross international borders. To our sur-prise he rips off the exoskeleton and sucks out the squishy flesh. We laugh and walk away. *Ciao, ciao...*

Olivia is homesick tonight, just three days into our ten-day trip, and it's hard to combat her longing for home along with my own. Her home-sickness, coupled with an irrational fear of robbery or harm in this very safe part of the city, causes her to fall asleep tonight weeping and leaves me on guard and hearing every sound in the neighborhood. We are safe, but are our loved ones? she has asked. What of Jack and Emma and Papa?

The third whammy for us is the lack of a telephone. I opted not to rent an Italian cell phone this time, thinking we could find Internet cafés and times to call home periodically. I'd rather spend the money on a gondola ride, I told Tim. What I didn't expect was this sense of being totally cut off from my family—and from help, should we need it. We in America are used to total access and communication all the time. We freak when our cable goes out for half a day, much less our phone service.

Don't get me wrong. When it's not very late at night, Olivia and I are having a very good time. Today we saw the oldest church in Venice (c. AD 636)—on a largely abandoned outer island, the birthplace of this ancient city. Tomorrow we go to a Vivaldi concert in another ancient church in the heart of the city. We'll cross the canal and tour a monastery and bell tower with a famed view of Venezia. And I'll have time to write, and Liv will have time to read...and we'll suffer through our homesickness with chins held high and shoulders back. (Yes, yes, poor us. I can hear you...)

But you do hear what *I am* saying, right? That we are all vulnerable just beneath the surface. Being in a strange place where people speak another language, far from our family and creature comforts—this has simply stripped away the layers of protection that normally cover up our everyday vulnerabilities. It has left us naked and raw, wincing at any glancing blow.

I put Liv to bed tonight, praying that God will protect me and mine. That He will set His angels before us and behind us and on every side. That we will be brought together again before we know it, a family once more. And I tell Liv that God does not send us a spirit of fear but of courage. That we are not to wallow in the darkness but believe in the light. I waited until her tears subsided and her breathing became slow and even.

And then I rose. To write out my own feelings and listen to the harmless noises of a cozy Italian neighborhood on a Saturday night. A soccer team tossing a ball back and forth. Two other people stumbling home after one too many glasses of wine. A couple walking hand in hand...and I hear laughter.

Protector God, thank You for this adventure in a foreign land. Sometimes I feel vulnerable even at home, and I thank You for this reminder of what it means to be cowering and in need of You. Make me brave, Lord, courageous. Infuse me with Your strength, and bathe me in light. Drive away the shadows, Jesus. In You, I am all I need to be. In You, I find strength when I am weak. Praise Jesus! Praise Jesus! Praise Jesus! I find strength in praising You. I discover again that You are present, right here, with me. Praise You, Father. Praise You. Amen.

What Is God Saying to Me in This?

_____

_____

_____

Making the Scripture Mine

Psalm 34:4–8 is very reassuring, confident, hopeful. I love the line about an angel making a protective circle about me. I can almost see him in my mind's eye, arms and wings around me, tucking me beneath his chest, sheltering me. While the Bible does not teach about individual guardian angels, it does teach that the Lord surrounds and protects His people.

Read the passage again slowly, as if you were the writer. How would you state the message to best apply to your life?

_____

_____

_____

Pray, "Father, show me what You want me to learn in this passage." Now reread the verses and finish this sentence: God wants me to…

_____

_____

_____

My Prayer

_____

_____

_____

24

A Grand Day Along the Grand Canal

But make sure that you don't get so absorbed and exhausted in taking care of all your day-to-day obligations that you lose track of the time and doze off, oblivious to God. The night is about over, dawn is about to break. Be up and awake to what God is doing! God is putting the finishing touches on the salvation work he began when we first believed. We can't afford to waste a minute, must not squander these precious daylight hours in frivolity and indulgence... Get out of bed and get dressed!

ROMANS 13:11–14

I'm happy to report that our home-sickness has passed, like a wave of nausea, washed away overnight. After sleeping in and being awakened by the sound of bells tolling on our busy street, we arose to a day that was slightly cooler, slightly less sticky. Liv had found her equilibrium again, and I felt stronger, ready to encourage her forward.

Things on My Mind

Concerns, to-do lists, grocery lists, whatever—get these things down here so you can concentrate for the next ten minutes.

_____

_____

_____

We went to a museum in a palace on the Grand Canal, ate prosciutto sandwiches, and rode home on the busy number-one *vaporetto*, a water-bus stuffed with tourists. Halfway back to our stop, we even snagged a couple of seats in the back, out in the open. We returned to our apartment, and I got some good writing done while Liv worked on her journal and scrapbook. Then we made ourselves a supper of tortellini and peppers and dashed out the door to a Vivaldi concert, held in a four-hundred-year-old *scuola* and performed by virtuosos in eighteenth-century garb and powdered wigs.

I'm enjoying sharing my travel diary with you, yes. But my point is that last night Liv and I were afraid and quivering in a corner, feeling that what we should really do was get our buns on a plane home, where we belonged, where we felt safe and known. Today we had our "sea legs" again, knowing who we were—treasured children of God covered by His grace— and enjoying everything He had set before us. As we ate our dinner tonight, we shared a shocked moment when we realized we only have a few days left; our vacation is rapidly dwindling away. So much to do! So much to see! Olivia said, "We probably won't even want to go back on Friday."

How our perspective can change in such a short time! I seem to learn this lesson over and over again in life: when life seems dark, hold on until daybreak. My R.N. mother says that patients everywhere will tell you that nighttime is the worst. Everything seems harder in the still of the night— pain seems to deepen; fear seems to pierce our foggy brains; imaginations run wild. But in the daytime, it all is more easily negotiated.

Are you facing a "night" right now? Sometimes "nights" can last for days, weeks, even months. But hold on, baby. Dawn is on its way. Pray for it. Trust in it. Hold on. You just might have your own magnificent day as soon as you wake up, get up, and reach for it.

Father, You are so good to me. Forgive my narrow-mindedness and fear and folly. I'm here now, again, where You want me, grounded in Your truth rather than swirling in the devil's lies. Keep my eyes on You, Lord. Help me focus. Amen.

What Is God Saying to Me in This?

_____

_____

_____

Making the Scripture Mine

While Paul, in Romans 13, is speaking of the dark as the present age—the time before Jesus returns—and of the light as when Jesus does return, we may apply the truth of his words to our much smaller scale of day-to-day life. If we are to live each day as if Jesus were already beside us, as if every hour counts, then we are literally leaving the dark to walk with the Father of light.

Read the passage again slowly, as if Paul were kneeling before you, beseeching you to understand the magnitude and importance of his words. How would he put it to you?

_____

_____

_____

Pray, "Father, show me what You want me to learn in this passage." Now reread the verses and finish this sentence: God wants me to...

_____

_____

_____

My Prayer

_____

_____

_____

_____

_____

25

How Wide Your Window?

Go out into the world uncorrupted, a breath of fresh air in this squalid and polluted society. Provide people with a glimpse of good living and of the living God. Carry the light-giving Message into the night so I'll have good cause to be proud of you on the day that Christ returns.

PHILIPPIANS 2:15–16

Yesterday Olivia and I toured a da Vinci exhibit in an old Venetian church along the Grand Canal. They had set up one contraption after another, on a small scale, so people could try them out. It was fascinating to see da Vinci's mind "in action," in everything from ideas about flight to drills to armament. One of the last exhibits was a floodlight, which was a simple box with a candle set inside. Because of a rounded lens on the opposite side of the box, the light was cast in a greater area. It's the same scientific principle used today in floodlights.

Things on My Mind

Concerns, to-do lists, grocery lists, whatever—get these things down here so you can concentrate for the next ten minutes.

My thought was this: we're all boxes, boxes with a candle inside. Some of our glass lenses are small; some are wide. Some are even wider, having a large convex lens that allows for more light to shine. The goal, of course, is to have the widest, roundest lens possible in our boxes. But the light starts with the candle.

We want a nice candle with a long wick, a wick that will light quickly and throw a bright flame dancing upward. We want some airflow that allows the flame to breathe, dance, shine. The knowledge of Christ is our candle. The Holy Spirit is the air that flows over the flame, feeding it, bringing it life. No candle—no wick to light. No air—no flame. No window—no light.

It's a pretty common Christian image. But what I had not considered before was the nature of our windows. I like the idea that we need a wide window but also one that curves outward, reaching to our world in every direction possible, spreading God's light as far as possible. We're called to become transparent, shining Christ in open invitation to everyone who comes near. We're not supposed to be sputtering flames but rather floodlights.

I'm thinking my window is pretty wide right now but also pretty flat. I'm going to try to start pushing it out here and there over the coming months and years. Where do you find yourself? How wide? How round? How transparent?

Father of light, thank You for showing Your face to me everywhere I look. Thank You for pulling my window wider. I ask You for the guts to get "out there" more in the coming years. To know Your Word, to know You so well that I can do nothing but shine Your light. Use me, Father. Shine through me. Bring others closer. We all need You. Amen.

What Is God Saying to Me in This?

_____

_____

_____

_____

Making the Scripture Mine

The NIV translates Paul's words in Philippians 2:15–16 this way: "shine like stars in the universe as you hold out the word of life." What an image! Imagine yourself deep into the countryside on a moonless night with a sky full of stars. Imagine that you hold a lantern in one hand, the Bible in the other. Imagine your face aglow, inviting those lost in the dark to come near. You are a bright light in a dark world!

Take a moment to reread the passage from Philippians. How would you word the message for your life today?

_____

_____

_____

Pray, "Father, show me what You want me to learn in this passage." Now reread the verses and finish this sentence: God wants me to…

_____

_____

_____

My Prayer

_____

_____

26

Pregnant Robins

I've learned by now to be quite content whatever my circumstances. I'm just as happy with little as with much, with much as with little. I've found the recipe for being happy whether full or hungry, hands full or hands empty. Whatever I have, wherever I am, I can make it through anything in the One who makes me who I am.

PHILIPPIANS 4:11–13

Here in Colorado the robins are about to burst their feathers, they're so pregnant. Our friend Alicia just gave birth to her first child, Parker. And in cleaning out my purse, I found one of those pregnancy-test sticks that I've carried around ever since I got pregnant with Jack.

In the back of my makeup drawer, I found another—the first I knew of Emma. Olivia's stick is long gone, but I find myself clinging to these two with their bright pink double lines that signify Life and Joy and Surprise and Love and God to me. They represent how life can change in an instant—in irrevocable ways.

Things on My Mind

Concerns, to-do lists, grocery lists, whatever—get these things down here so you can concentrate for the next ten minutes.

_____

_____

_____

_____

What will today hold for me? for you? Will tragedy or unspeakable joy be around the corner for us? Every day is an adventure, and only one thing stays the same: our God who shelters us and keeps us and prepares the way for us—if we're looking to follow where He leads. And whether we are embracing glad tidings or terrible sorrow, God is present.

My life is never boring. Some days I long for boredom, routine, but I know that I wouldn't want it for more than a few days even if I could get it. Besides, I believe that if we're bored, we're not following God with all the energy we should. That we're not looking for signs of Him in every moment of every day. Once we're aware of our God who lives and breathes all around us, the God who whispers and shouts at us, the God who leads us forward into risking, challenging, hoping, dreaming, living with all the zest He has laid within our hearts… Once we are doing all that, there is no room for boredom.

You may not be growing round in the middle like the robins in our yard, heavy with child, but what does God have in store for you today? Your life can change radically in a day. Are you ready? Are you excited? Life is an adventure. It's time we live that way.

Lead me on, Lord. I am ready as long as You are near me. I need You and love You and want You with me every step of the way. I sing Your praises for how You've created me, and I wait with happy anticipation of what You will bring my way next. Prepare my heart, Father. Strengthen me. Through You, with You, we can do anything. Amen.

What Is God Saying to Me in This?

Making the Scripture Mine

To be fully equipped for a God-centered, God-led life, we need to find the central stability Paul speaks of in Philippians 4:11–13. Such hope! Such confidence! Such peace! He sounds fully ready to encounter glory or demise, as long as God is alongside him. He seems to casually say, "Bring it on. I'm ready."

Read the passage again slowly, as if you were writing the words yourself to other believers in a faraway land. How would you make the words your own, reaching out to the believers?

_____

_____

_____

Pray, "Father, show me what You want me to learn in this passage." Now reread the verses and finish this sentence: God wants me to...

_____

_____

My Prayer

_____

_____

_____

27

Hungry Babes on a Branch

GOD, the Master, The Holy of Israel,
has this solemn counsel:
"Your salvation requires you to turn back to me
and stop your silly efforts to save yourselves.
Your strength will come from settling down
in complete dependence on me—
The very thing
you've been unwilling to do."
ISAIAH 30:15

O ur fat robins, round with pregnancy, sit on plum branches just
sprouting delicate pink flowers. The
robins look intent on something. Nest-
ing, I soon see. I remember those last
days of pregnancy—needing to get
paint on the walls, the crib in order, the
correct number of onesies to feel *ready*.

This mother robin chooses to nest
right outside our upstairs window, and
I can see the two delicate, freckled, blue
eggs in her tightly woven home. She leaves them for only minutes at a time
and settles in when she returns with what seems to me a quiet satisfaction.
It reminds me of my granddad, alone on a dilapidated Montana farm,

---

Things on My Mind

Concerns, to-do lists, grocery
lists, whatever—get these
things down here so you can
concentrate for the next ten
minutes.

spending long spring afternoons watching a nest of robins in his own yard. I wonder if he had thoughts like my own. I remember that he was sad the spring there were no robins in his tree.

In a short time the babies arrive, two ugly little birds, first wet from egg slop, then inordinately fluffy with first feathers. But always, always they are crying out, beaks open, begging their mother to return with fat worms and round bugs to eat.

My friend Rebecca often describes us this way—like baby birds calling out to our Father in heaven, asking Him to fill us. We cry out for sustenance, for purpose, for filling. We cry out for covering, protection. We cry out for His presence. Crying out, squawking, always noisy.

As uncomfortable as this constant wanting is, as much as we endeavor to be quiet, peaceful Christians, squawking is exactly what our God wants from us. He wants us crying out to Him as often as possible, looking to Him for direction, provision, fulfillment. He wants to hear us cry out to Him for help on big and small things. It is His gig—the mother robin role. Coming to cover and warm us. Taking care of our day-to-day needs. And eventually showing us how to fly.

Father, I don't like to be dependent. I don't like the feeling of insecurity and need. I want to be on my own. So I try to fly before my wings are ready. Forgive me for racing ahead of You. Forgive me for constantly trying to take life into my own hands. Help me to settle into dependency on You, into trust and faith. Amen.

What Is God Saying to Me in This?

Making the Scripture Mine

At least I'm not alone. At least my ancestors all had the same issue—this constant desire to take care of everything ourselves, to ignore God. I'm a firstborn, always eager for responsibility, plans, structure. Waiting on God, depending on Him...hmm...that's tough for me. You too?

Reread Isaiah 30:15, and then read these verses that follow:

"You've said, 'Nothing doing! We'll rush off on horseback!'
    You'll rush off, all right! Just not far enough!
You've said, 'We'll ride off on fast horses!'
    Do you think your pursuers ride old nags?
Think again: A thousand of you will scatter before one attacker.
    Before a mere five you'll all run off.
There'll be nothing left of you—
    a flagpole on a hill with no flag,
    a signpost on a roadside with the sign torn off."

But GOD's not finished. He's waiting around to be gracious to you.
    He's gathering strength to show mercy to you.
GOD takes the time to do everything right—everything.
    Those who wait around for him are the lucky ones. (verses
    16–18)

Which phrases from Isaiah 30 leap off the page for you? Paraphrase them here:

_____

_____

_____

Pray, "Father, show me what You want me to learn in this passage." Now reread all the previous verses and finish this sentence: God wants me to...

_____

_____

_____

My Prayer

_____

_____

_____

Part 3

Summer

28

When Are We Gonna Get There?

This is GOD's Word on the subject: "As soon as Babylon's seventy years are up and not a day before, I'll show up and take care of you as I promised and bring you back home. I know what I'm doing. I have it all planned out—plans to take care of you, not abandon you, plans to give you the future you hope for.

"When you call on me, when you come and pray to me, I'll listen.

"When you come looking for me, you'll find me.

"Yes, when you get serious about finding me and want it more than anything else, I'll make sure you won't be disappointed."

JEREMIAH 29:10–14

Things on My Mind

Concerns, to-do lists, grocery lists, whatever—get these things down here so you can concentrate for the next ten minutes.

Paula Rinehart says in her phe-nomenal book *Strong Women, Soft Hearts,* "This is what each of us needs to be able to say, 'I am doing what I was born for.'" I love this because it's what every satisfied-this-side-of-heaven woman says—whether that means being a stay-at-home mom, finding one's particular gifting in ministry, or pursuing a God-ordained career. It should be our goal too. I think this is the driving force of *The Purpose-Driven Life*'s bestsellerdom; as a people, we long to find God's good purpose for our lives and the fulfillment that accompanies it.

We can ascertain where God is leading us through prayer, conversations with others who know us well, and sometimes trial and error until we "happen upon" something that brings us happiness. It's a process; it doesn't happen overnight.

Sometimes, however, in the process of trying to get to what we're born for, we get discouraged, dismayed, dissuaded. Satan doesn't like us on a track that will lead us to contentment, and he often sends discouragers, naysayers, and powerful persuaders our way, trying to keep us off God's best road for us. It is our job to stay on track, to pray for God's direction, and ignore the Enemy.

For me, it's the oft-agonizing *slowness* of the whole process that discourages me. I can see where I might get to someday and find inspiration in the vision, but I want to be close to the destination *now*. (Patience has never been one of my gifts.)

Our job is to keep on the path, putting one foot in front of the other, forever taking steps forward, concentrating on the path rather than how long it's going to take to reach our goal. (Can't you hear your kids in yourself? A plaintive wail from the backseat crying, "When are we gonna get there?") Eventually we'll find some satisfaction and peace in the journey itself. Our heart's hope is that we get to live with that satisfaction.

I draw peace from envisioning Moses setting one foot in front of the other through the wilderness (we won't dwell on the fact that he spent forty years trudging forward); his direction ultimately led his people to the Promised Land. I find inspiration in Noah, who for decades sawed a board, hammered a nail, and eventually ended up with an ark; his dedication preserved humanity. Paul journeyed far and slept in prison cells to do what he was born for; his teaching gave us much of our New Testament foundation.

If those three can do what they did, surely I can keep on the road God has laid before me...

Father God, thanks for instilling in me Your calling, Your hope, Your desires for me. Help me find what I was born for and find peace in the vision as well as the journey. Take care of me, Lord Jesus. Protect me, as You have promised to do. Thank You for always walking alongside me as I wait on Your perfect timing. Amen.

What Is God Saying to Me in This?

the path is rough, but it's your path.   7/2/15

Making the Scripture Mine

Jeremiah 29:10–14 speaks to God's people in their exile from Jerusalem to Babylon, encouraging them that there will be an end, a day when it all comes together again. But seventy years! Can you imagine waiting for anything for seventy years??? I like the verses that precede this passage too. In Jeremiah 29:4–9 God basically tells His people to keep living, even in exile—to marry and have babies, to chase peace and prosperity, to pray, to seek God's true Word. *Life doesn't stop in the waiting time...* It goes on. And good things are around the corner!

Read the passage again slowly, as if the old prophet Jeremiah were writing to you alone, in this day, in this place, seeing you in your private struggle. How would the aged man phrase his message for you?

Pray, "Father, show me what You want me to learn in this passage." Now reread the verses and finish this sentence: God wants me to...

_____

_____

_____

My Prayer

_____

_____

_____

29

Dependence Day

> May God himself, the God who makes everything holy and whole, make you holy and whole, put you together—spirit, soul, and body—and keep you fit for the coming of our Master, Jesus Christ. The One who called you is completely dependable. If he said it, he'll do it!
>
> 1 THESSALONIANS 5:23–24

It's July 5, and last night we were at a family party watching fireworks above a small town to the north and the Air Force Academy to the south. As we watched bursts of red and blue and gold flower in the sky and dissipate, we all smiled, feeling the stirrings of national pride and the thrill of spectacle.

Now I am a very strong woman of Scottish-Norwegian-German heritage. I can stand on my own two legs just fine, thank you very much. I'm surprised when other women are taken aback by what I've done on my own—whether it's traveling to Niagara Falls

Things on My Mind

Concerns, to-do lists, grocery lists, whatever—get these things down here so you can concentrate for the next ten minutes.

or Alaska—and I wonder why they don't hop on a plane to do it themselves. I'm surprised when people are impressed by my ability to lead, because it seems natural to me, second nature.

But what hits me on July 5 is that God doesn't want my independence. He likes my strength, my gumption. But what He *wants* is my dependence on Him.

It chafes, this knowledge. Nothing feels more secure than relying on myself. I fully know what I'm capable of, what I can and cannot accomplish. God? Let's face it, in human terms, He's rather iffy.

To be clear, I know that God can do all things. I've seen His work; He is alive and well in my own life. He just doesn't always do what I want Him to do or when I think He should do it. And learning to trust Him and depend on Him day in and day out is a long, hard road for me.

But our Lord *is* dependable. He has led me and rescued me in wild ways throughout my life, and as I age, I recognize Him in action more and more. He is amazingly trustworthy and faithful to me, to you. And I take it as a personal call to submit to His methods, His timing, on a daily, weekly, monthly, annual basis. To become dependent upon Him for my very life.

Lord, You know I don't like submission. Even when I've seen that You are totally trustworthy, it's hard for me not to wrestle back the reins of my life. I sigh as I pray this, exasperated with myself, wondering if You're rolling Your eyes about me right now. Thanks for remaining with me, sticking with me, even though I don't deserve You. Thank You for grace, for forgiving me. Thank You for molding me into who You want me to be. I adore You, Father. You are my thoroughly dependable God, and I submit my life to Your care. Amen.

What Is God Saying to Me in This?

_____

_____

_____

Making the Scripture Mine

Paul wanted the Christians in Thessalonica to fully grasp the future—the Second Coming of Christ—in order to better shape their present. That truth is important for us today as well; we believe we'll get to meet Jesus face to face in this life or the next. But if you're like me, you forget it in the day to day.

If we keep that truth front and center, waiting for Jesus to return at any hour, then we remember that we're not "all that"—that only He is "all that." This truth cuts out all the garbage that fills my days, all the pride and greed that fill my heart, and it points me to the One who makes me whole.

Read 1 Thessalonians 5:23–24 again slowly, as if Paul were writing to you. How would you paraphrase the scripture for your life today?

_____

_____

_____

Pray, "Father, show me what You want me to learn in this passage." Now reread the verses and finish this sentence: God wants me to…

_____

_____

My Prayer

_____

_____

_____

Wilted Flowers

If God gives such attention to the appearance of wildflowers—most of which are never even seen—don't you think he'll attend to you, take pride in you, do his best for you? What I'm trying to do here is to get you to relax, to not be so preoccupied with *getting*, so you can respond to God's *giving*. People who don't know God and the way he works fuss over these things, but you know both God and how he works. Steep your life in God-reality, God-initiative, God-provisions. Don't worry about missing out. You'll find all your everyday human concerns will be met.

MATTHEW 6:30–33

O kay, so I bought a ton of perennial flowers yesterday and got twenty-seven of thirty-one little bundles in the ground the same day (patting self on back). Today the remaining four were in various states of decline, acting as if my delay had sent death knells through their tender stems and they were already saying good-bye to loved ones… I forged ahead, planting three more today; the last looked too sad to

---

Things on My Mind

Concerns, to-do lists, grocery lists, whatever—get these things down here so you can concentrate for the next ten minutes.

_____

_____

_____

even attempt the transfer. But you know what I'm facing… Anyone who has gardened knows that if flowers are wilted in the pot, they'll have a tough go in the ground.

I dug up the dirt and prepared the soil around each spot where I would plant a flower. I lined the holes with Miracle-Gro dirt, gently pulled the flowers out of their containers, and loosened their roots. I set them in the holes and surrounded them with more Miracle-Gro. I watered (intensively). I stood there, hoping they'd perk up immediately. No luck.

The next morning one-third are looking more dismal, one-third are looking about the same, and one-third are looking as bright and perky as A-1 Nursery flowers.

The flowers remind me of how we are with God. Sometimes we feel rather wilted, worn out, and on our way out. We feel dry, starved. And then God sends us an overwhelming shock of water and food and hope, and we have three choices: die, continue suffering, or suck it up and bloom.

The lesson is this: God gives us what we need, when we need it— whether we recognize it or not. We can choose to ignore His provisions and die, continue on in our woe-is-me mode, or drink it in and take it for all its worth—relishing the wealth before us.

So…where are you? I've definitely had dying days, suffering days, and blooming days. I want to choose to bloom. God is shining His light. He sends down a gentle shower of rain. He surrounds me with vitamin-rich soil. I just need to find the means to draw it all in.

Father God, forgive me for ignoring all You give me when everything seems dry. I face certain days as I would a death squad, ignoring that You shield me and give me water and sustenance. I face other days just carrying on as if I were in a tiny plastic pot rather than set free in the great, wide world for growth. Lord, I want to bloom each day, my face to You, my arms lifted up. Help me, Jesus. Amen.

What Is God Saying to Me in This?

_____

_____

_____

Making the Scripture Mine

Since Jesus Himself said these words in Matthew 6:30–33, how can we ignore them? Why are we so quick to dissolve into doubt and fear rather than trust that God will provide what we need, when we need it?

Read the passage again slowly, as if Jesus were walking arm in arm with you, encouraging you with each word. How would you rephrase the scripture for your life today?

_____

_____

_____

Pray, "Father, show me what You want me to learn in this passage." Now reread the verses and finish this sentence: God wants me to...

_____

_____

_____

My Prayer

_____

_____

_____

31

Stinky Feet

This, in essence, is the message we heard from Christ and are passing on to you: God is light, pure light; there's not a trace of darkness in him.

If we claim that we experience a shared life with him and continue to stumble around in the dark, we're obviously lying through our teeth—we're not *living* what we claim. But if we walk in the light, God himself being the light, we also experience a shared life with one another, as the sacrificed blood of Jesus, God's Son, purges our sin.

If we claim that we're free of sin, we're only fooling ourselves. A claim like that is errant non-sense. On the other hand, if we admit our sins—make a clean breast of them—he won't let us down; he'll be true to himself. He'll forgive our sins and purge us of all wrongdoing.

1 JOHN 1:5–9

Things on My Mind

Concerns, to-do lists, grocery lists, whatever—get these things down here so you can concentrate for the next ten minutes.

_____

_____

_____

_____

Just so you know I'm not telling any secrets, my husband told me I could write this. Tim, as fabulous and wonderful as he is, has a terrible case of stinky feet that comes on with the heat of spring and summer. Every year.

We're not talking mild foot odor. We're talking blue cheese, soak-the-feet-every-night, place-shoes-in-the-garage, fumigate-the-family-room kind of stinky feet.

The other night I reeled backward and looked at him with wide eyes. "Ooo, Tim. You need to do something about *that*."

He looked at me and gave me a sheepish, impish smile. He wrinkled his nose and said, "They kind of smell good to me."

We laughed together and later talked about how stinky feet could be a metaphor for sin in our lives. Some of our sins, once we live with them long enough, smell sweet to us even if they're foul in the nose of God. We turn them around in our head and heart until we can justify them, even honor them. We like them!

But if we're smelling them as fervently as a police dog chasing a convict, then we know our sins for what they are: stinky feet. My Stinky Feet sin is pride. It's one thing to have healthy self-confidence, another to have false humility. I'm working on it. Let me assure you, God is working on it with me. I've had several experiences in the last few years that are sure to humble me for decades to come.

What's your Stinky Feet sin? Jealousy? Anger? Gluttony? Greed? What is it? It's there. You just have to smell it out as God does.

Smell me, Lord, and give me Your sense of smell to sniff out the sins in my life. Don't let me revel in them, turning them in my mind into something good rather than the foul things they are. Pry them out of my life, Father. Help me recognize them and repent of them. I claim strength in You, Jesus. Amen.

What Is God Saying to Me in This?

_____

_____

_____

Making the Scripture Mine

The passage in 1 John speaks of a vital concept for each of us: living in communion with God. What does it mean to "live in communion" with the Holy? It means a dynamic relationship, not static. And in John's words, we can leave the wide, warm avenue of light, fully covered by God, and enter a self-deluded alleyway of darkness where danger lurks. Gut-level honesty, owning up to our sins, and confessing them keep the communication flowing. Confession reminds us that He is God and we are no more than humble followers, constantly taking dark alleyways away from Him and then stumbling back to His side.

Read the passage again slowly, as if John were holding your hands and urgently whispering to you so you might fully absorb every word. Which phrases speak most to you right now? Write them out here:

_____

_____

_____

Pray, "Father, show me what You want me to learn in this passage." Now reread the verses and finish this sentence: God wants me to...

_____

_____

_____

My Prayer

_____

_____

_____

32

Camp Anxiety

Be agreeable, be sympathetic, be loving, be compassionate, be humble. That goes for all of you, no exceptions. No retaliation. No sharp-tongued sarcasm. Instead, bless—that's your job, to bless. You'll be a blessing and also get a blessing.

1 PETER 3:8–9

My girls head off to camp today. Liv is eleven; Emma, eight. Liv will spend a week at Rainbow Trail; Emma, three days. They've both been to camp before, but they were still suffering pangs of fear last night. *What if I get there and nobody likes me? What if I don't like them? What if I'm all alone?*

In many ways I still go over these same questions in my head anytime I go to a new place alone. As a married person, mother, business partner, and friend, I rarely have to do this. Even in airports or on buses, 85 percent of the people I pass are talking on a cell phone, listening to music, or walking with someone else. People wish to appear connected or ward others off

Things on My Mind

Concerns, to-do lists, grocery lists, whatever—get these things down here so you can concentrate for the next ten minutes.

_____

_____

_____

with earphones that subtly say, "Don't bother me. I'm in my own connected world." We go to great lengths to avoid uncomfortable silences and stares, to avoid the awkwardness of not knowing what to say to a stranger or how to reach across the chasm.

Because it's hard work, isn't it? And it brings out our vulnerabilities and fears. We're beset by thoughts of not being good enough, attractive enough, interesting enough.

While I'm comfortable putting words on paper, I'm not so good with out-loud words. I edit my thoughts continually, and sometimes when I let them out, they are not half as interesting or profound or encouraging or funny as I had hoped. There's no chance to rewind, edit. My constant fear is that I'll appear foolish.

It's silly pride that makes me dwell on such things. And I work on trusting in the goodness of humankind rather than fearing people's judgment. We all judge others constantly, but Jesus' dream is that we would see Him in everyone else. If we did that, would we not love better, reach out more, hope? Would we not say, "He is in you! He is in me! We are family already; there are no strangers here"? Would it not give us an overriding sense of encouragement, familiarity, comfort, joy?

God has all kinds of gifts to give us when we begin looking for Christ within everyone else. If we see each person as His special creation just as we are His special creations, we operate out of kindness rather than judgment, courage rather than fear. And in the process, we discover a broader spectrum of friends than we've ever had before.

This is what I'll tell my daughters when we drop them off at camp today: treat others the way they'd like to be treated; look for the little girls we prayed for—the ones who will be their special camp friends. And on an adult scale, it will remind me to keep my eyes open for people whom God is planting in my life—women I need to know and who need to know me. There's a world of sisters out there for us, girls. Let's go find 'em.

Father, You know that it's hard for me to risk, to trust enough in others to reach out. But that's what You call us to do—to constantly reach out, love, and bless, even if our efforts are rebuffed. Give me Your courage. Give me Your strength. Give me Your optimism. Give me Your insights. Thank

You for the dear friends I have. Help me always be on the lookout for others You have yet to bring near, women with whom I would connect as a "heart friend." Help me be open to the ways they can teach me and the ways I might encourage them. Let us be You to one another. Amen.

What Is God Saying to Me in This?

_____

_____

_____

Making the Scripture Mine

Peter was a natural leader among the disciples (he's always listed first), and it's obvious he got this faith thing down. Peter put Jesus first and foremost in his life and became the "boldly confident and humbly self-effacing servant of Jesus Christ...a compelling witness to what he himself describes as 'a brand-new life, with everything to live for.'"[5] His letter is written as an apostle on assignment, sent to all Christians, already scattered wide.

Read 1 Peter 3:8–9 again slowly, as if you were picking up a letter from Peter written only to you. How would you reword the scripture for your life today?

_____

_____

_____

Pray, "Father, show me what You want me to learn in this passage." Now reread the verses and finish this sentence: God wants me to...

_____

_____

My Prayer

_____

_____

_____

_____

_____

_____

33

Thirty-Six Miles from Camp

Satan's angel did his best to get me down; what he in fact did was push me to my knees. No danger then of walking around high and mighty! At first I didn't think of it as a gift, and begged God to remove it. Three times I did that, and then he told me,

My grace is enough; it's all you need.

My strength comes into its own in your weakness....

Now I take limitations in stride, and with good cheer, these limitations that cut me down to size—abuse, accidents, opposition, bad breaks. I just let Christ take over! And so the weaker I get, the stronger I become.

2 CORINTHIANS 12:7–10

Things on My Mind

Concerns, to-do lists, grocery lists, whatever—get these things down here so you can concentrate for the next ten minutes.

We left the house, fully packed and double-checked, the girls ready for a few days at camp other than jittery with adjustment fears. We drove an hour and a half over the first foothills of the mountains, laughing, talking, en route to the glorious Rainbow Trail Lutheran Camp...and then our car sputtered and died.

No cell-phone coverage. No one stopping to help. The closest business a river-guide outfit half a mile back. Ninety-seven degrees. Three kids. Two heartbroken girls realizing they would not hit camp in time to choose their counselors or their cabin or meet others who might become friends... You get the picture.

My hubby, Tim, headed back to Dvorchak's River Guides to use their phone, reestablish our AAA coverage (I had failed to pay the bill), locate a tow truck on a Sunday, and call an auto-repair center. I stayed back to deal with girls in tears, a confused toddler, and the heat radiating in waves at the side of the road. Emma slumped into a ball on her seat. Liv walked off a few paces to hide her tears.

I let them grieve a little and then said, "I know this is hard. I know this is not what you had in mind. But the lesson in this is one that will serve you the rest of your life. If you can let go of what might have been, what you wanted, and instead make the most of what is; if you can trust that God will somehow make this right, you'll be better off."

In a little while we were able to talk about how God could use the day for their greater good. Maybe they'd get the nicest counselor in the camp (one they might not have chosen). Or maybe there was another little girl in each of their cabins who needed them or who would prove to be a new friend (and they might not have ever met!).

I talked them through things I have to talk myself through, week after week. I'm constantly coaching myself to make room for God to move, to live aloud in my life rather than be stifled by me. Sometimes this is hard. Sometimes it stretches me in ways I don't wish to be stretched. But in the end it is always good, because God is good. All the time.

Father, thank You for granting me some wisdom in my life and the vision that You are alive and well in every hour of my day regardless of what I face. Help me recognize stress and trouble as opportunities for You to minister to me, to teach me, every time. Help me embrace such days with immediate joy and faithfulness. I long to be worthy in this way. Amen.

What Is God Saying to Me in This?

_____

_____

_____

Making the Scripture Mine

My *NIV Study Bible* says of 2 Corinthians 12:9: "Human weakness provides the ideal opportunity for the display of divine power."[6] So even though our weakness makes us uncomfortable, even though we'd rather avoid pain and strife, if we make room for God in the midst of it, we have the opportunity to observe the Divine at work.

Read this passage again slowly, as if you were listening to Paul yourself. How would you paraphrase the scripture for your life today?

_____

_____

_____

Pray, "Father, show me what You want me to learn in this passage." Now reread these verses again and finish this sentence: God wants me to...

_____

_____

_____

My Prayer

_____

_____

_____

34

Sunset Blooms

Then Jesus went to work on his disciples. "Anyone who intends to come with me has to let me lead. You're not in the driver's seat; *I* am.... Follow me...."

...Jesus took Peter and the brothers, James and John, and led them up a high mountain. His appearance changed from the inside out, right before their eyes.

MATTHEW 16:24; 17:1–2

Things on My Mind

Concerns, to-do lists, grocery lists, whatever—get these things down here so you can concentrate for the next ten minutes.

_____

_____

_____

I'd forgotten what this feels like. I hear nothing but the constant hum of an air conditioner and the muffled, dim hum of traffic fourteen floors down. There's no toddler pulling on my legs, nobody saying, "Mama, Mama, Mama..." I stare and stare out at the silver cast of Lake Erie and the wide flat of the horizon.

I've intentionally come on this business trip a day early to grab some desperately needed writing time. (Can you say three book deadlines at once?) Two days ago I was in the mountains of Colorado in Newly Repaired Vehicle, picking up Youngest Daughter from camp. Today I am in Buffalo, New York, watching a brilliant, glowing red sun set over the western flats. It's only missing a twin sun to match a scene in *Star Wars*.

Watching it sink until it disappears and remembering the red suns of my California childhood calms me. The sky settles into the dusky grays and lavenders and rose blushes of postsunset, and still I stare, as if I can't absorb it enough, as if I'm trying to memorize it.

I am like a dry sponge. A desert flower thirsting for rain.

And then I realize I've become a Mom Hard to Pry Away.

My friend Missie and I used to talk about such women and wonder at the fact that it was hard to pry them away from family and everyday life for even a couple of days of retreat. We would dis the women who could not trust husbands with children and schedule in order to take time for themselves and their God.

It's not that way with me. My husband is fully capable. He'll pick up Eldest Daughter tomorrow from camp and even show up with Toddler and Youngest Daughter in tow in time for worship prepickup time. He's that way. Faithful. Awesome. My man. But it's me... I'm the one who feels like she's barely holding on, craving time to come together as a family around the dinner table, relaxed, laughing, conversing. Instead, it feels like we're always "managing"—managing schedules, responsibilities, behavior, consequences. There's a layer of stress that I'm desperate to peel away, leaving us the happy family I see inside.

But as a Mom Hard to Pry Away, I've forgotten this sense of peace. This place where I can be silent and pray and listen, really listen, for the Savior to speak. He is active, vital in my life, and yet I give Him precious little room to move closer and talk to me. And if I can't remember the basics of spiritual life, how good will I be at unleashing the family I see just beneath the layer of stress and schedule to be all they were created to be?

I must begin with me, first and foremost. If I can get it down, if Tim can get it down, if we can prioritize our days to spend time just with God, we'll be better models for our children. Jesus called men away from families, work, schedules—everything—to follow Him. He said, "Follow me," then turned away, never expecting the fishermen behind Him to do anything but follow Him. Those men walked away from homes, boats, tomorrow's 4:00 a.m. to noon fishing shift—all to follow the Savior who called.

So who are we to question Him? Who are we to say, "No thanks. I can't take the time. I'm too important. I can't trust what will happen to my house, children, laundry…whatever"? Would we really say such silly, trivial, self-centered things to our Savior?

God is calling each of us, this day, to come away and spend five minutes, five hours, five days with Him. And nothing—nothing—is more important than that.

I'm speaking to you, Mom Hard to Pry Away, (and you know who you are)—and I'm speaking to myself. God calls. If He is Priority Number One to us, to our husbands, and to our children (whether they know it or not), can we afford to say, "Maybe later, Father"? Think about it for a second. If Jesus Christ were right here before you now, asking you to come away for a time and abide with Him, would you be able to say no?

Retreat? Vacation? An afternoon in a park while the kids spend two hours with a friend? Find your space and commit it to God. He'll do the rest.

Father, what is my deal? Why am I so wrapped up in how I do things at home that I think it will all fall apart without me? Why do I not trust You and my husband or others to make it work? I trust if You call, You will watch the people precious to me, left behind because of my desire to answer Your call. You've asked me to come here, to spend time with You, to be quiet. Cleanse me, Lord. Forgive my self-importance and lack of humility. Make the most of this time. Speak to me, Father. I am here, waiting. I long for You. I call to You. Come, Lord. Come! Amen.

What Is God Saying to Me in This?

_____

_____

_____

_____

Making the Scripture Mine

Eugene Peterson says, "Matthew provides the comprehensive context by which we see all God's creation and salvation completed in Jesus, and all the parts of our lives—work, family, friends, memories, dreams—also completed in Jesus. Lacking such a context, we are in danger of seeing Jesus as a mere diversion from the concerns announced in the newspapers. Nothing could be further from the truth."[7]

Read Jesus' words in Matthew 16:24; 17:1–2 again slowly, as if He were speaking to you alone. How would He say this to you right now?

_____

_____

_____

Pray, "Father, show me what You want me to learn in this passage." Now reread the verses and finish this sentence: God wants me to...

_____

_____

_____

My Prayer

_____

_____

_____

35

A Place Called Home

> Yes, because GOD's your refuge,
> the High God your very own home,
> Evil can't get close to you,
> harm can't get through the door.
> He ordered his angels
> to guard you wherever you go.
>
> PSALM 91:9–11

I'm a Montana girl, born in a picturesque valley in its northwest corner. While I didn't grow up there, I spent every summer of my life on one of its lakes. I am flying in now for my annual trek, like a woman on a pilgrimage.

I wrote a novel awhile back that I'm reminded of now as the trees and mountains become recognizable even from the air. In that novel I set my characters on my beloved lake and wrote about things that only an insider would know—how the wind blows its

Things on My Mind

Concerns, to-do lists, grocery lists, whatever—get these things down here so you can concentrate for the next ten minutes.

_____

_____

_____

peaceful waters into fierce whitecaps on days that will be glorious and how the best days come after the summer people retreat and the lake is again a peaceful paradise, the domain of fishermen rather than Jet Skis.

After that book released, I heard from people around the lake who had picked up the book or been given a copy. They loved that sense of connection, understanding. Others wrote wishing they could go to a place that sounded so lovely. Staring at the cover from far away, I did too.

Montana is where I find rest, healing, peace. It's where I'm most aware of my surroundings, be they the shadow of a mountain or a curve in the lake's shore. It's where I feel complete, centered. It's home.

Undoubtedly, you have a place like that. A place that makes you smile wistfully when you think of it, or maybe you're fortunate enough to live there. Some people find this sense of home even in a place they lived in for only a short while. But the point is, they know it.

In this same manner we are to know Christ. We're supposed to feel so at ease in His company that we miss Him when we're distant, much as we miss home. We're supposed to make our way back to Him when we've been gone for a while. And He's always there, waiting, eager to welcome us no matter how far or how long we've wandered.

When we're at home with Christ, He settles into our living rooms, cooks in our kitchens, and helps us take out the garbage. He even nestles in with us in the bedroom, in that most intimate of places, so we can trust Him more than any other, day in, day out. He opens His arms and whispers, "Come home, beloved. Come home to Me."

Father of my heavenly home, I want You to be my new home base. No matter where I am, I want to know I am at home with You. I want that sense of peace and completeness and healing that I get, wherever I am, in connecting with You. Help me remember that You are close by, waiting to shelter and protect and nourish me. Amen.

What Is God Saying to Me in This?

_____

_____

_____

Making the Scripture Mine

Psalm 91:9–11 is a tender and reassuring passage. We're all at home in God's house—whether that means in a church or out in the world; wherever we are, we are claimed by Him. We are at home.

Read those verses again slowly, as if the psalmist were writing to you alone. How would he put his message to best speak to you?

_____

_____

_____

Pray, "Father, show me what You want me to learn in this passage." Now reread the verses and finish this sentence: God wants me to…

_____

_____

_____

My Prayer

_____

_____

_____

36

Fresh Paint

If we claim that we're free of sin, we're only fooling ourselves. A claim like that is errant nonsense. On the other hand, if we admit our sins—make a clean breast of them—he won't let us down; he'll be true to himself. He'll forgive our sins and purge us of all wrongdoing. If we claim that we've never sinned, we out-and-out contradict God—make a liar out of him. A claim like that only shows off our ignorance of God.

1 JOHN 1:8–10

Today I'm stripping delicate blue flowers off my walls and covering sunny yellow paint. I'm taking down lovely eyelet curtains and replacing them with more sophisticated, long white panels. Last month in Jack's room I stripped Beatrix Potter wallpaper and replaced it with a manly taupe. This month I'm on to the girls' rooms.

My children are growing up, longing to have rooms that reflect their choices rather than mine. I'm inserting my own persona to a certain extent, guiding Middle Daughter away from fuchsia to smoky lavender, Eldest

Things on My Mind

Concerns, to-do lists, grocery lists, whatever—get these things down here so you can concentrate for the next ten minutes.

Daughter from neon green to icy aloe. Their rooms are changing, and we all know what that means for Mama—some work.

And yet the work is welcome, with its promise of nice results just around the corner. It's amazing what a coat of paint can do for a room. I cover up old marks from furniture and pen with one swoop. In seconds I see what change can occur with a simple act. Just pour, dip, and roll.

Isn't this much like our inner lives? If we will only give God full rein in our lives, He can paint our rooms faster than anything we've ever seen. With a simple bowed head, acknowledgment of the scars, and a request to cleanse us, change us, it's done. What color is your room when He's finished? Bright yellow? Sky blue? Rosy red?

Only we stubbornly remember the marks just beneath the paint. God sees only our new color, fresh hope. The challenge is to adopt the new color, accept it as the new beginning it is. God offers us total forgiveness. Holding on to the marks beneath the fresh coat of paint is a transgression itself. Accept His healing. Accept His fresh coat of paint.

Savior, I know You throw my sins away as far as the east is from the west, but it is difficult for me to let them go, to forget. I punish myself for past sins as if I could do Your saving work for me. Help me let them go. Help me accept Your forgiveness as clearly as a white wall accepts a coat of colored paint, letting it seep into every nook, every cranny, erasing the marks and mars in my wall. I hand my memories over to You. I hand them over to You on a daily basis, if need be. And I accept the new color You've painted me. Amen.

What Is God Saying to Me in This?

_____

_____

_____

Making the Scripture Mine

At the time that John was writing the letter that is 1 John, the Gnostics and their heresies were in full swing. Verse 1:10 specifically addresses the Gnostics of his day and their denial that their immoral actions were sinful. Hmmm...doesn't that sound a lot like our present-day culture? Even we Christians would rather explain away our actions than acknowledge our sins, ask God's forgiveness, and find healing.

Read 1 John 1:8–10 again slowly, as if John were whispering to you the great secrets of the Christian life. How would you paraphrase the scripture for your life today?

_____

_____

_____

Pray, "Father, show me what You want me to learn in this passage." Now reread the verses and finish this sentence: God wants me to...

_____

_____

_____

My Prayer

_____

_____

Laugh Tracks

Up with God!
Down with his enemies!
Adversaries, run for the hills!
Gone like a puff of smoke,
like a blob of wax in the fire—
one look at God and the wicked vanish.
When the righteous see God in action
they'll laugh, they'll sing,
they'll laugh and sing for joy.
Sing hymns to God;
all heaven, sing out;
clear the way for the coming of
    Cloud-Rider.
Enjoy GOD,
cheer when you see him!
          —PSALM 68:1–4

I was heading into the Christian booksellers' convention and riding the escalator when I first noticed it. Laughter. It took me a couple more rides up and down the silver stairs to recognize what I was hearing. Piped in male and female voices. Chortles and guffaws, giggles and belly laughs. Some

Things on My Mind

Concerns, to-do lists, grocery lists, whatever—get these things down here so you can concentrate for the next ten minutes.

_____

_____

_____

_____

faint, some louder, like real people. Quiet enough that if you weren't paying attention, you wouldn't notice it. Subtle enough that you'd think it was people, either a few steps down or up from you, having a good time.

The psychology of it is pretty obvious. Heading into a giant convention center, one braces for impact—aching feet, tired mind, sore jaw from talking all day. But if you're heading into something upbeat and happy, you instead feel invigorated, stimulated, intrigued, welcomed. As if you're going to a party!

I can see how laughter affects my kids. When our house is full of laughter, we all feel better and interact better. When there is no laughter, life seems like drudgery. I want our home to be filled with giggles and guffaws. When my children open the door, coming home from school or a friend's house, I want them to feel the joy.

Is our home always like that? No. Nine times out of ten, my hubby and I are madly trying to get something done—work, dinner, a task. I'm loathe to admit that instead of welcoming them with a big smile and open arms, I often treat my kids as an intrusion, another thing on my list I have to deal with. I found myself this week, in the middle of summer vacation, wishing for the coming school year, for a quiet house that stays somewhat together, for kids separated from each other instead of arguing with each other, for the girls to be gone from eight to four. *Yuck.* Even as I write that, I feel conviction wash over me.

Day-to-day life can be difficult. We busy moms maneuver through complicated schedules and daily grinds that can be just that—a grind. But when we allow our daily lives to fall into such a pattern, when we bark at our children instead of talk with them, when we walk around with grim faces rather than a ready smile, we give the Enemy what he wants.

Joy is a choice. Every morning when we wake, we choose to encounter the day as something to be survived or something to be welcomed. On this day I choose joy. I'll hear that goofy escalator laugh track in my head and choose to smile. I'll choose to see my kids as God in action and let it stir my heart to praise. And I will do so again tomorrow, and the next day. And gradually the laugh tracks will become my normal mode rather than a training tool in my head. And the grind will become *life* again.

> *Father of joy, forgive me for succumbing to the survival mode. There is so much to do and too little time to do it in, but I don't want to live life this way. Even when I'm busy, I want my children to hear me laughing. I want to laugh with them. Restore the joy in our home, and help me to model it. In Christ's name. Amen.*

What Is God Saying to Me in This?

_____

_____

_____

Making the Scripture Mine

Psalm 68 is a rich treasure to be mined. In this song that would have been sung as a processional, David wrote of God's triumphs from Mount Sinai (where Moses received the Ten Commandments) to Mount Zion (Jerusalem). Glory! Triumph! Honor! Joy!

Read the passage again slowly, as if you were in the midst of a crowd, everyone honoring your God. Better yet, think of Jesus Himself entering your home (along with a hundred others, leaving throngs outside, and everyone shouting His praise). How would you word the scripture for your life today?

_____

_____

_____

_____

Pray, "Father, show me what You want me to learn in this passage." Now reread the verses and finish this sentence: God wants me to…

_____

_____

_____

My Prayer

_____

_____

Don't See Me

Investigate my life, O God,
find out everything about me;
Cross-examine and test me,
get a clear picture of what I'm about;
See for yourself whether I've done anything wrong—
then guide me on the road to eternal life.

PSALM 139:23–24

I turned from the kitchen sink yesterday, noticing that Jack, my three-year-old, had flushed the toilet for the third time in a row. The bathroom door was open, and I tipped my head in to see what was going on.

Jack was ripping up toilet paper into tiny pieces and dropping them into the basin, then turning to flush.

"Jack…," I began.

His eyes widened, and then he thrust out his chin and a hand toward me. "No! No, Mama. Don't see me!"

Things on My Mind

Concerns, to-do lists, grocery lists, whatever—get these things down here so you can concentrate for the next ten minutes.

_____

_____

_____

How often do we wish that God would not see us in the act of sinning? How often do we know we are sinning and yet hope He will look away, because we find perverse pleasure or thrill or entitlement or stature from doing so?

Jack is under my desk as I write this. He's saying, "Mama, I not doing anything," which means, of course, that he is doing something he shouldn't. In our household, the age of three is a year of exploring boundaries, testing boundaries.

Being almost forty, I'm not often bold enough to tell God that I'm not doing anything when I know very well that I am. But I am childish enough to hope God won't see me. Or desperate enough to recognize my sin after it is committed and hope that God will look away.

This is futile, obviously. Of course He saw me. And He will not look away. We stand under His gaze every hour of every day. He loves us. He wants to teach us. He wants to curb us from our sins before they are committed. He wants us to grow up in our faith and live like Him. Little by little—and by His grace—I get closer every day.

See me, Lord. Cover me with Your gaze, and expose my sins to my own eyes before I commit them. Wash me clean. Forgive me. Make me Yours, wholly. I long to belong to You and honor You in everything I do. See me, Lord. See me. Amen.

What Is God Saying to Me in This?

_____

_____

_____

Making the Scripture Mine

The psalmist's complete vulnerability in Psalm 139 makes me think of a woman staring up at the sky, naked, arms open wide, so thoroughly trusting her God that she can stand before Him without looking away, without covering up. Vulnerable. Assured of His love. Open.

Reread Psalm 139:23–24, this time aloud, as if you were writing the psalm. Change the words if you stumble over them; make them your own. What does the passage say to you? How would you reword the passage for your life today?

_____

_____

_____

Pray, "Father, show me what You want me to learn in this passage." Now reread the verses and finish this sentence: God wants me to...

_____

_____

_____

My Prayer

_____

_____

_____

Down Deep

A white-tailed deer drinks
from the creek;
I want to drink God,
deep draughts of God.
I'm thirsty for God-alive.
I wonder, "Will I ever make it—
arrive and drink in God's presence?"
I'm on a diet of tears—
tears for breakfast, tears for supper.
All day long
people knock at my door,
Pestering,
"Where is this God of yours?"
                    PSALM 42:1–3

Things on My Mind

Concerns, to-do lists, grocery lists, whatever—get these things down here so you can concentrate for the next ten minutes.

_____

_____

_____

At the lake in Montana where we spend part of every summer, the water can be bone-chillin' cold. Fed by melting glaciers and snow and mountain rivers and creeks, our lake rarely reaches more than seventy degrees, and that's just the top nine or ten inches.

If you dive into the lake in May, it's

so cold that the muscles in your limbs will contract in protest. You'll get hypothermia if you stay in longer than ten minutes. In June the lake starts to warm up a little, but it's hardly swimming water. You're still looking at canoes and kayaks as your friends. In July you have a chance of swimming, particularly toward the end of the month. In August too. During those few weeks at the apex of the summer's heat, you can dive in and gasp at the cold but then get somewhat used to it. The trick is floating or trying to swim in the top nine to twelve inches of water, where the sun has done its good work for you.

Below that thermal layer, the water gets chilly. You can handle it for a bit, but there's enough of May's hypothermic promise to keep you from diving down too often.

I think my faith is like that. I hope my upper layer is getting deeper and deeper as I grow older and learn more. But too often I only let God heat my top layers. I'm comfortable with the chill down deep, comfortable with my sins that I really don't want Him to address, thank you very much.

And too often my Savior has to reheat water that He warmed up before. I let a big, chilly blast ("cold spots" we call them in swimming) of a deep current wash away the good work He's already accomplished.

I want to get to the place where I'm a big Jacuzzi of hot water. I don't want to live my life divided. I want God to have worked through every layer of my waters and have made me His own on every level. I don't want to let a cold current undo His good work. I want to stand strong, pushing it to the side, around me, past me.

I want God to do His good, deep work in me.

Through and through, Jesus. I want You to work through me, then through me again, driving out the cold waters of sin. I want You to warm my waters, helping me combat the Enemy, who brings chill and fear into my life. I want languid, peaceful waters that have been through Your gates and warmed by Your Son. Go deep in me, Father. Go deep. Amen.

What Is God Saying to Me in This?

_____

_____

_____

Making the Scripture Mine

Psalms 42 and 43 form a prayer for deliverance from the Enemy and for restoration of God's presence in His temple. The deer, potentially hunted by the enemy, thirsts for the water of life. These psalms, ascribed to the sons of Korah, appear to have been written by a liturgist—someone whose job was to lead worship. And now he's far from home, hunted, away from his beloved temple. What relevance does this have for us?

Until we get to heaven, we'll face constant separation from our God. We are in "enemy occupied territory," as C. S. Lewis once noted. We are hunted and besieged, and the Enemy wants us to do anything but discover the Holy Spirit within us, around us, strengthening us, protecting us, empowering us.

Read Psalm 42:1–3 again slowly, as if you were once in charge of leading music in your own magnificent, beloved church but now are in a far-off country. How would you word the scripture for your life today—and how do the pestering questions make you feel?

_____

_____

_____

Pray, "Father, show me what You want me to learn in this passage." Now reread the verses and finish this sentence: God wants me to...

_____

_____

_____

My Prayer

_____

_____

_____

Part 4

Fall

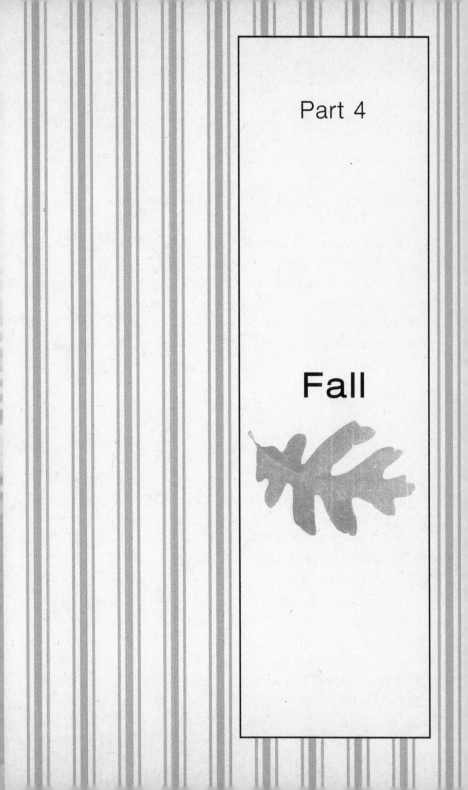

40

For Love or Money

Stay on good terms with each other, held together by love. Be ready with a meal or a bed when it's needed. Why, some have extended hospitality to angels without ever knowing it! Regard prisoners as if you were in prison with them. Look on victims of abuse as if what happened to them had happened to you. Honor marriage, and guard the sacredness of sexual intimacy between wife and husband....

Don't be obsessed with getting more material things. Be relaxed with what you have. Since God assured us, "I'll never let you down, never walk off and leave you," we can boldly quote, "God is there, ready to help; I'm fearless no matter what. Who or what can get to me?"

HEBREWS 13:1–6

Things on My Mind

Concerns, to-do lists, grocery lists, whatever—get these things down here so you can concentrate for the next ten minutes.

Today *Good Morning America* had a segment about how money is the number-one bone of contention for couples. I had been thinking about Rosa, our Compassion International child, and how I'd love our kids to meet her and understand how life is in the third world—to truly realize how great we have it. Her picture is posted on our refrigerator—a fridge/freezer that we could eat out of for weeks—and I once learned that Rosa's mother's daily prayer is that she will have enough milk for each of her children.

This weekend we'll attend a silent auction to help fund our church youth's mission trip to Puerto Rico. Another group is going to Milawe, Africa. I happened upon an in-depth *Time* magazine article about a three-year-old Milawe boy who died because his bed did not have a net treated with insect repellant. The most disheartening thing about the article? The nets cost $1.50. For the cost of a soda at McDonald's, this child could still be bringing smiles to his parents' faces.

When I read that article, I immediately thought about Jack, who is approximately the same age, and what grief would cover our family if we lost him. But African children die all the time of malaria or starvation or other ailments that could be cured. Yet I still obsess about the need for new carpet, landscaping, clothes, a car. I place those things ahead of the world and even my own church.

My wise, wonderful friend Sarah says, "I'm pretty sure God won't give us any more money to handle until we show Him we can handle what we have." It's been rough these last years, taking a hiatus from writing, building a company, and living on one income, yet the tight financial situation has brought me more clarity than ever before about what money is to be used for and what it is not. I now know that debt is bondage, and I do not want to remain forever tied to it.

I also heard on the news that the average person is now retiring with $50,000 in savings and only $50,000 of equity in their homes. While this shows some initiative in savings, there is no way that amount of money will carry a person through retirement. What will happen to that generation? Who will care for them? for us? We, as a country, have some challenges ahead. We Christians must prepare. We must get our affairs in order. God is calling us to lead the way.

So I am determined to help increase our giving to 10 percent within the next two years, to get out of debt, to save money for retirement and college, to give money for things like bed nets, to send kids on mission trips (that eventually my own kids will go on), and then to live within what remains. Because that is how God wants it. And how my husband wants it. And if the two most important guys in my life are happy, maybe I will find peace in that place too.

Lord, I am so thankful for what You have given me. I am awed and amazed at Your generosity and grace. Thank You for food on the table and clean water from our faucet. Thank You for screens that keep out the bugs and a country that has so much—from roads to parks to schools. Help me keep my eyes on how You want me to handle the money You give me; help me honor You first and then spend on things You would approve. I am weak, but You are strong, Lord. I trust You with this aspect of my life too. Amen.

What Is God Saying to Me in This?

_____

_____

_____

Making the Scripture Mine

I love how the author of Hebrews gets down to brass tacks and is so thoroughly practical in chapter 13! Keep in mind that at the time, being "ready with a meal or a bed" was a pretty serious suggestion. With few inns available, travelers relied upon the kindness of strangers. Talk about trusting your life to your Lord!

Read verses 1–6 again slowly, as if the author of Hebrews were writing specifically to you, reminding you how to find or stay on the right road. Which phrases speak the most to you today?

_____

_____

_____

Pray, "Father, show me what You want me to learn in this passage." Now reread the verses and finish this sentence: God wants me to...

My Prayer

41

Breathing Room

At the time GOD made Earth and Heaven, before any grasses or shrubs had sprouted from the ground—GOD hadn't yet sent rain on Earth, nor was there anyone around to work the ground (the whole earth was watered by underground springs)—GOD formed Man out of dirt from the ground and blew into his nostrils the breath of life. The Man came alive—a living soul!

GENESIS 2:5–7

We Christian women are generally hyperventilating. We are running so fast and in so many directions that it's hard to find a moment to unwind, let alone stay still and listen for God. We breathe shallowly and fast, seeming to brace for the day-to-day impact of life, clenching our stomachs as if we're going to get punched.

Genesis 2:7 says God breathed life into Adam, just as He does for count-less babes born each day. From the moment He breathes life into our lungs, He longs for us to concentrate on Him, to listen for His voice. He longs for us to come away with Him

Things on My Mind

Concerns, to-do lists, grocery lists, whatever—get these things down here so you can concentrate for the next ten minutes.

_____

_____

_____

every day, even for just a few minutes. When we stop and take some deep breaths, we relax. Our circulation is better with more oxygen in the blood. We think with greater clarity. This clears the way for focused time with God.

In the Bible, particularly in Eugene Peterson's paraphrase, *The Message*, you can see all kinds of people breathing like us: When the queen of Sheba saw the splendor of Solomon's palace, "it took her breath away" (1 Kings 10:5). Throughout the trials of Job—perhaps because he seems on the brink of death for months on end—there are many instances of breathing: "He won't even let me catch my breath" (9:18); "You gave me life itself, and incredible love. You watched and guarded every breath I took" (10:12); while Elihu lectures Job, he pauses to take "a deep breath" (36:1), then later speaks of the wonders of God's awesome power, the very witness that "the High God roars in the thunder.... I'm stunned, I can't catch my breath" (36:33–37:1). Even God Himself, after the arduous week of creation, is described as stopping and taking "a long, deep breath" (Exodus 31:17).

Psalms, too, in contemplation and wonder, refers to more peaceful and wondrous breathing: "you let me catch my breath" (23:3); "Take a good look at God's wonders—they'll take your breath away" (66:5). Disgusted with the faithless, David asks his Lord to "knock the breath right out of them, so they're gasping for breath, gasping, 'GOD.' Bring them to the end of their rope, and leave them there dangling, helpless. Then they'll learn your name: 'GOD,' the one and only High God on earth" (83:15–18).

We might be faithful, but life is knocking the breath out of us. Or, if we're honest, we may be unfaithful, forgetting for days, weeks, months at a time that God is the Lord of our lives. God calls us to take the time to just be with Him. At the worst moments, He has to let us dangle at the end of our ropes, as David describes. Then we realize we're missing...our Savior.

I've started looking for breathing moments. I've found them in a few extra minutes in the shower, in taking the long way home from an errand when I'm alone in the car (and can pause somewhere remote and quiet), and even in my driveway, singing a rockin' praise song to Him (with or without the radio). Find stolen moments for your Savior. And breathe.

My God on High, I need some breathing room. I'm not breathing as You want me to; I'm spending too much time holding my breath or bracing for impact rather than calming myself, listening for You. Show me where I can grab a few minutes of breathing room each day. Help me hear You and what You have to say. Teach me. Mold me. Make me Yours. And fill me to capacity with the breath of life. Amen.

What Is God Saying to Me in This?

_____

_____

_____

Making the Scripture Mine

Genesis is where it all begins. Our Scriptures. Our story. Our very lives. We tend to skim over Genesis's verses, feeling that they do not have as much relevance for us as the New Testament does. But there are important things to glean from every chapter of the Bible. What is God trying to say to us here?

Read Genesis 2:5–7 again slowly, as if you were translating the text from an ancient language. Dig deep. How would you rephrase these words to have the greatest relevance for your life today?

_____

_____

_____

Pray, "Father, show me what You want me to learn in this passage." Now reread the verses and finish this sentence: God wants me to…

_____

_____

_____

My Prayer

_____

_____

_____

42

Back to School

Be assured that from the first day we heard of you, we haven't stopped praying for you, asking God to give you wise minds and spirits attuned to his will, and so acquire a thorough understanding of the ways in which God works. We pray that you'll live well for the Master, making him proud of you as you work hard in his orchard. As you learn more and more how God works, you will learn how to do *your* work. We pray that you'll have the strength to stick it out over the long haul—not the grim strength of gritting your teeth but the glory-strength God gives. It is strength that endures the unendurable and spills over into joy, thanking the Father who makes us strong enough to take part in everything bright and beautiful that he has for us.

COLOSSIANS 1:9–12

Things on My Mind

Concerns, to-do lists, grocery lists, whatever—get these things down here so you can concentrate for the next ten minutes.

I was one of those freaky kids who loved going back to school. I loved the promise of a new year—of new teachers, new notebooks, new textbooks, new pencils and pens. I loved the whole learning process, particularly when I was challenged. It was like New Year's Eve for me—everything heavy with potential.

My children, unfortunately, do not share my freakishness. My girls tend to be anxious about making friends, getting nice teachers, and entering new classrooms. Even new school supplies fail to inspire them adequately. They lament the return to routine and homework (I don't blame them for that).

But the fact is, life is all about learning. When we cease to learn, we cease to grow. God calls us to constantly seek out others who will teach us and inspire us. We do best when we are listening to people who make us think—be they authors, radio broadcasters, television hosts, pastors, Bible-study leaders, or brothers and sisters in the faith. We're to surround ourselves with people who build us up, not tear us down, and who help us explore the complexities of living a life of faith in a fallen world.

Too often we refuse the call to go back to school. We shut down our learning centers, preferring instead our comfortable cocoon of mindless television and the pablum in our magazines and books. (Okay, okay, I confess to reading *People!* You are not alone!)

But just as we watch the sugars in our diets, we should indulge in the mind and heart candy carefully, always pushing for solid nutrition that will fortify us, build us up inside. And to do that for our minds and hearts, we have to adopt a learner's attitude, always seeking ways to grow.

Abba Teacher, show me what I need to learn on a daily basis. Make me a learner, pliable in both heart and mind. Train me in the way You wish I would go. Take me back a grade if I need to go back. Then teach, show, enlighten me. Amen.

What Is God Saying to Me in This?

_____

_____

_____

Making the Scripture Mine

Paul wrote the Colossian letter to baby believers in Colosse (present-day Turkey). They were troubled by off-kilter teaching and were struggling to stay on the right path and grow in the right way.

Imagine you're a brand-new Christian believer in a far-off country. It's likely that your only written references to the faith are Old Testament writings and letters from Paul and your fellow believers. Any written word is a sacred reference for you, to be studied, to be ingrained in your heart and mind. Read Colossians 1:9–12 again slowly, as if you're picking up a page of a letter Paul wrote only for you. How would he tailor these words for you? Write them here:

_____

_____

_____

Pray, "Father, show me what You want me to learn in this passage." Now reread the verses and finish this sentence: God wants me to...

_____

_____

_____

My Prayer

_____

_____

_____

43

Disappointment's Gift

Here's the story I'll tell my friends when they come to worship,
and punctuate it with Hallelujahs:
Shout Hallelujah, you God-worshipers;
give glory, you sons of Jacob;
adore him, you daughters of Israel.
He has never let you down,
never looked the other way
when you were kicked around.
He has never wandered off to do
    his own thing;
he has been right there, listening....
Down-and-outers sit at GOD's table
and eat their fill.
Everyone on the hunt for God
is here, praising him.
"Live it up, from head to toe.
Don't ever quit!"...
Babies not yet conceived
will hear the good news—
that God does what he says.

PSALM 22:22–24, 26, 31

Things on My Mind

Concerns, to-do lists, grocery lists, whatever—get these things down here so you can concentrate for the next ten minutes.

_____

_____

_____

_____

My ten-year-old, Olivia, loves drama and has been involved in many plays at our church, even landing lead roles. She went out for the big fifth-grade play, *Aladdin,* hoping for at least a narrator part, and I know, in her heart of hearts, she hoped for the lead role of Jasmine.

She was put in the chorus, along with most of the other kids. For those with a flair for the dramatic, this is the equivalent of being a forced pick when dividing up teams. She wanted that lead role—she could taste it, it was so close—not some nameless, no-line role...

I told her that it's hard when we're judged "lesser than" in a public forum. That the important thing is to focus on what she does have—a part in the play, an opportunity to learn more about drama, a chance at fun—rather than on what she doesn't. But I well remember losing a role in a play called *Kismet* and how I longingly wished I had the lead rather than being stuck in the harem! Now, as an author, I peruse the bestseller lists wistfully, wishing I were in that upper tier that gets named month in and month out.

The reality is that we're incredibly blessed right where we are. Even if Liv had the role of Jasmine, she'd encounter other issues—figuring out the time to do homework, dealing with the envy of others. If I were on the bestseller list month in and month out, my pressures might increase rather than decrease. Because I'm only listed occasionally, I think I work harder to always produce the best book I can. If I had already "arrived," would I cave in to mediocrity?

Okay, I confess that I'd like the challenge of being a consistently best-selling author. But sometimes disappointment is the best gift we can be given. It keeps us humble and helps us remember that God is in charge and we aren't. We must focus on what is good in each day, on what God has given us, rather than on what the world keeps from us. The world is imperfect, but God is not. God adores us and does what He promises. If we can concentrate on that truth and trust it, we can work through any disappointment.

Lord, I struggle with disappointment. Not just disappointment about what I can do with my gifts but on other fronts as well. Help me see You in the midst of every day, to focus on the fact that You are alive and well in my life no matter how dark the day seems. I know You have my best interests at heart. Sometimes, I confess, I doubt. Forgive me, Father, and help me see my world through Your eyes. Help me sense Your presence even in the sorrow. Amen.

What Is God Saying to Me in This?

_____

_____

Making the Scripture Mine

The psalms are excellent in their work of shifting focus off ourselves and back onto our Maker. Spend some time in the book of Psalms, and you'll find that the psalmist at times laments his situation but that, to a greater extent, he keeps his eyes on God, as if he needs to remind himself that his Lord is still there, still worthy of praise, still the Alpha and the Omega, the beginning and the end.

The psalms remind me that God is eternal and that, by comparison, my life here is brief and only in Him will I find eternal glory. Praising Him eases my temporary slights and pains as I refocus on greater goals.

Which phrases jump out at you today? Paraphrase them here:

_____

_____

Pray, "Father, show me what You want me to learn in this passage." Now reread the verses from Psalm 22 and finish this sentence: God wants me to...

_____

_____

_____

My Prayer

_____

_____

_____

44

Hold Fast

Why would you ever complain, O Jacob,
or, whine, Israel, saying,
"GOD has lost track of me.
He doesn't care what happens to me"?
Don't you know anything? Haven't you been listening?
GOD doesn't come and go. God *lasts*.
He's Creator of all you can see or imagine.
He doesn't get tired out, doesn't pause to catch his breath....
Those who wait upon GOD get fresh strength.
They spread their wings and soar
    like eagles,
They run and don't get tired,
they walk and don't lag behind.
          ISAIAH 40:27–31

Sometimes faith becomes more physical than spiritual. Some days life batters us with a wind so strong that it threatens to steal our very breath. Our challenge on those days is to hold fast against the storm...and, like a skilled sailor, to actually use its force for good.

Things on My Mind

Concerns, to-do lists, grocery lists, whatever—get these things down here so you can concentrate for the next ten minutes.

If we are good sailors, we have a ship with a finely crafted keel that extends deep beneath us, carving through the water and keeping us from capsizing. We have a strong, pointed bow that can take the deepest wave and emerge atop it. We have well-kept ropes that will not unravel. We have a wide, strong helm where we can find a firm foothold—lashing ourselves to the wheel if necessary, a wheel that points our ship in the right direction.

There are times when we use the storm to go faster by raising up all our sails and riding the force of the storm. There are times when we lash our sails to the mast and crossbeams and pray for survival through the battering. There are times we ride out the storm the best we can.

We hold fast through the storm. We hang on to all that we know is true and right and good. We cling to it, using our backs and our arms and our wrists and our fingernails. We hold fast to our God, who promises never to leave us or abandon us. And when we do, the storm eventually passes.

Winston Churchill said, "If you're going through hell, keep going." The point is not to languish in the storm. Even if you've lashed all your sails through the gale, you'll know when it is time to unfurl at least a few to get moving again. You inherently know—as if you can read the waves deep below or the skies high above—when the worst of it is past, and though you are battered and bruised, it's time to move forward.

Sometimes faith becomes more physical than spiritual. Our goal is to build our ships strong and true. To keep them in good shape so we can weather any storm. We may emerge from the tempest with cracked boards, snapped lines, or even a broken mast, but the point is to emerge. To hold fast against the storm and then listen for the Lord to tell you to move again.

Sometimes faith becomes more physical than spiritual. Hold fast. Hold fast. Hold fast.

Father God, help me care for my spiritual ship during fair-weather days so I can weather any storm. Help me trust You, my shipbuilder, to fashion the best keel, the best bow, the best stern, the best sails, the best ropes, the best helm. Shape me into the best sailor possible so I can take on any storm, able to hold fast to You during the worst of it. And use the storms to make me stronger. Please, Lord, use those stretching storms for Your good, my good. In Jesus' name. Amen.

What Is God Saying to Me in This?

_____

_____

_____

Making the Scripture Mine

When I was in college and my first real boyfriend broke my heart into a thousand pieces, Isaiah 40:27–31 was the passage that sang to me. It was the first time Scripture really rose, took shape, entered my ears and heart. It was the first time I realized that the Word is alive, that it had relevance for me, thousands of years after it was written.

Read the passage again slowly, as if Isaiah were speaking to you like a big brother irritated with his little sister. How would you paraphrase the scripture for your life today?

_____

_____

_____

Pray, "Father, show me what You want me to learn in this passage." Now reread the verses and finish this sentence: God wants me to...

_____

_____

_____

My Prayer

_____

_____

_____

_____

_____

45

I Think He Can

Some of you wandered for years in the desert,
looking but not finding a good place to live,
Half-starved and parched with thirst,
staggering and stumbling, on the brink of exhaustion.
Then, in your desperate condition, you called out to GOD.
He got you out in the nick of time;
He put your feet on a wonderful road
that took you straight to a good place to live.
So thank GOD for his marvelous
    love,
for his miracle mercy to the children
    he loves.

PSALM 107:4–8

Things on My Mind

Concerns, to-do lists, grocery lists, whatever—get these things down here so you can concentrate for the next ten minutes.

_____

_____

_____

It's a rough day. Too much to do, too little time to do it in. You're tired— exhausted, in fact. You're needed by too many people, big and small. There's not enough of you to cover it all. Or if you give the 150 percent they demand, you'll be a pile of noodles on the floor. There are bills due, shopping to get done, piles of laundry, and beneath those dirty clothes, a filthy floor. You were supposed to be out the door half an hour ago, and your hair's still wet, and you don't have your makeup on. All you want to do is go back to bed and shut out the world.

I've had days like this, sister. I've actually thought (rarely, thankfully) that it would be kind of nice to go to prison or spend some time in the hospital, because (a) I would get some sleep, (b) I would be taken care of, and (c) no one would expect anything from me. Total-Demand-Removal Fantasy. I know, I know, it's terrible! Nobody in her right mind would ever wish for either of those things, right?

I usually laugh at myself for such insane thoughts and work to figure out what's freaking me out and what I can do to get back to Sane Lisa. Usually Insane Lisa gets into such pit thoughts because she's wallowing in a mantra of I-can't-do-it-I-can't-do-it-I can't... You get the picture. (And no, I'm not detaching here, referring to myself in the third person; I'm trying to make a point.)

To return to Sane Lisa (and someone my husband and kids can live with), I have to battle back with a second mantra, one I learned from a childhood book: I-think-I-can-I-think-I-can. The power of belief feeds us courage and strength. If we honestly believe we can do all things through Christ, who strengthens us, then we will! With that in mind, the mantra should be I-think-*He*-can-I-think-*He*-can...

So I stop for a moment and ask God to remind me of all that's good in my life. I start with the basics: food, shelter, love, light. Sometimes I write them all down. Try it yourself. Think basics. (Don't go big.) Things you have today that you appreciate. Things that will help you cope with the day. Things that will renew your sense of hope, awaken the sense of strength that Christ gives you.

Jesus, through You, I can do all things. But I need You today, Lord. I cannot do it all. I don't even want to. I want to run away from the pressures, the frustrations, the fear. Shelter me, Father. Help me take on one thing at a time this day. Help me see You working in me and even through these things that are all screaming at me at once. Cast away the Evil One, the one who plagues me and brings me down like a weight when I'm trying to swim. Cast him away. Help me concentrate on the freedom and hope I have in You. With You, one thing at a time. With You, one thing at a time. With You, one thing at a time. Amen.

What Is God Saying to Me in This?

_____

_____

_____

Making the Scripture Mine

Are you half-starved on a desert road, or are you on a good road today? The Israelites knew desert roads. Having traveled on the dusty desert path for forty years, they had a firm grasp of the real terrors of the desert. They knew the Arabian Desert as a boundary, as something only merchant caravans would brave. While most of us will never have to brave a real desert, we sometimes have "desert experiences" in which our very lives are at stake.

Read the passage from Psalm 107 again slowly. How would you paraphrase the psalm to best fit your life and needs today?

_____

_____

_____

Pray, "Father, show me what You want me to learn in this passage." Now reread the verses and finish this sentence: God wants me to...

_____

_____

_____

My Prayer

46

Maestro Moms

The rich and poor shake hands as equals—
GOD made them both!
A prudent person sees trouble coming and ducks;
a simpleton walks in blindly and is clobbered.
The payoff for meekness and Fear-of-GOD
is plenty and honor and a satisfying life.
The perverse travel a dangerous road, potholed and mud-slick;
if you know what's good for you, stay clear of it.
Point your kids in the right direction—
when they're old they won't be lost.

PROVERBS 22:2–6

I'm worried. Yesterday one daughter came home saying her best friend doesn't want to be her friend anymore. The day before, the other daughter came home in tears, saying a boy called her a name. Today my toddler stubbornly held on to a butcher knife (he pulled it out of the dishwasher) when I pleaded with him to let it go.

I'm afraid one's too tender, one's too prickly, one's too stubborn. I'm afraid life will be too hard for them...

Things on My Mind

Concerns, to-do lists, grocery lists, whatever—get these things down here so you can concentrate for the next ten minutes.

that they'll grow up to be people who don't know how to live life the easiest way until they're old. I don't want them to struggle. I want them to know love, laughter, success, peace, significance. And I want them to know it earlier rather than later.

Sure, I had to learn some things about dealing with life and people "on the job." But as mothers, we want to protect our babies, to smooth the way for them. And while Scripture seems to blithely say *just point the way, and it will be okay,* I have a hard time trusting that.

We are in on the most intimate parts of our kids' lives. We clean their ears, wash their sheets, wipe their rear ends, and cut their toenails. We watch them grow—day to day—from babes to toddlers to little children to preteens to teens to grownups. As the maestro of their sweet orchestra, we want to direct them all their lives so that when they're done practicing, theirs will be the finest music ever heard.

Can you hear me sighing? We all know life isn't like that. You can be the maestro, but your tuba player over there may refuse to practice. Your cellist might encounter a couple of broken strings that have to be fixed. A mammoth bug might fly into a flute, clogging a hole and disrupting the tune.

God wrote the music. He knows what it's supposed to sound like. And if we send our children in the right direction—if we teach them about how God is always there for them, how Jesus will always cover them with His grace, that the Lord's way is the smartest way—eventually they'll grow up to be amazing adults with Big City philharmonic sound. Some will figure it out at eighteen. Others at eighty. But it all boils down to them and God. Moms can only try to set the tempo…

Father, I'm afraid for my children. I ask You to show me now how to train them up right, how to give them the tools that will make life easier and more fulfilling. I don't want them to struggle or face pain because of poor choices, but I know that isn't in my control. Help me focus on what I can do now and give their futures to You. Thank You for the gift of each child—the miracle of Your creation. Help me remember that You knew them before they were born and that Your plans for them are plans for good. Amen!

What Is God Saying to Me in This?

Making the Scripture Mine

I tend to read Proverbs as a list of wise sayings more appropriate for other, wayward people than for my pulled-together self. But when I come off my high horse, I hear and see the wisdom anew. I see that the words are something for me to learn and relearn and relearn again.

Read Proverbs 22:2–6 again slowly, as if a wise old woman were imparting great knowledge to you, as if it were your task to write every word down because others were counting on you. How would she say these words from Proverbs to you so you could understand them?

Pray, "Father, show me what You want me to learn in this passage." Now reread the verses and finish this sentence: God wants me to...

My Prayer

_____

_____

_____

_____

47

Mama Told Me There'd Be Days Like This

A Message from Israel's GOD-of-the-Angel-Armies: "When I've turned everything around and brought my people back, the old expressions will be heard on the streets: 'GOD bless you!'...'O True Home!'...'O Holy Mountain!' All Judah's people, whether in town or country, will get along just fine with each other.

I'll refresh tired bodies;

I'll restore tired souls."

JEREMIAH 31:23–25

Oh yeah. You know what I'm talkin' about. Husband on day four of some weird ailment and unable to get vertical. Nine-year-old freaking out over being late to basketball practice. Six-year-old vomiting for the third time...on me. Man ringing the doorbell, and I'm still in my p.j.'s. Two phones ringing at the same time. Toddler wanting to be *home* and screaming in car for half an hour after we've lugged

Things on My Mind

Concerns, to-do lists, grocery lists, whatever—get these things down here so you can concentrate for the next ten minutes.

sister to basketball practice and sleepover. Empty fridge. House with exploding contents. (Will it ever be picked up and stay picked up again?

Ever?) Hours of work behind me, hours of work ahead. Missing cash card. Fast-food beverage spill in car. Mortgage bill appearing that was due…yesterday. Mm-hmm. Yep. You get the picture.

On days like this I have awful thoughts. I want to trade it all in. Be single. Be childless. Move somewhere exotic. Be free. My heart stops for a second as I write these words, but they're true. To have time to take a leisurely bath without wailing or gnashing of teeth outside my door… To pick up the house and have it stay clean for more than a few hours… To spend money on a manicure instead of another pair of kids' gloves destined to be lost in some snowbank… To find order and silence and time for me… Grown-up movies! Order! Control! A french-fry-less vehicle! Aaahhhh…

Tough, difficult days make us long for what we don't have. In our pointy little heads, we think that if we had what someone else has, everything would be all right. But after a decent night's sleep, we realize that if we had what they had, we'd have a whole other set of challenges that we'd gladly trade back for our own. It often appears better, easier, happier…over there.

Life isn't like it was in Eden. My daughter says in frustration, hands on hips, "Ooo! Why did Adam and Eve have to *eat* that apple, anyway?!?" She thinks that if they hadn't eaten the forbidden fruit, we'd still be in that idyllic place, healthy, happy, content. Could be. Or maybe Adam and Eve's great-grandchildren would've succumbed. Or had the torch been passed to me, I probably would've been munching on that fruit. God made us fallible, susceptible to weak, ungodly thoughts. Longing for more, longing for different. And on days like this, sometimes the only thing to do is pray for a change of attitude and a good night's sleep.

Because tomorrow is a brand-new day. And I'll smile when my kids are crawling all over my husband and me, burrowing under our blankets, pulling the sheets out, lugging stuffed animals in, flopping over me, interlocking ankles, giggling. Sunlight will stream through the window and set their catawampus hair afire in an angelic glow. My toddler will give me a too-wet kiss with huge, puckered lips, not caring about morning breath. And I'll think, *I wouldn't want any life but this one.*

Father God, thank You for preserving me through this day. Thank You for helping me keep generally calm in the chaos and not totally lose it with my kids. You've seen that before! Thank You for helping me choose to laugh rather than cry. And thank You for giving me hope for tomorrow. Give me a good night's sleep, Father. Deep. Peaceful. Restorative. Help my children rest long and hard and awaken healthy and happy and ready for a better day. Thank You for being present, right here in this crazy house, Lord. Thank You for every member of my family and for this day, as hard as it's been. And thank You for loving me even when I have less-than-pleasing thoughts. Amen.

What Is God Saying to Me in This?

_____

_____

_____

Making the Scripture Mine

Okay, you have a pretty good glimpse of how some days can be pretty darn tough for me. I'm guessing you can relate. But Jeremiah, the Old Testament prophet called to tell God's people of impending doom, knew real stress. This guy spent year after year screaming, "Woe to you!" at the top of his lungs. I'm guessing he wasn't very popular. But God moved him to speak, and he spoke, prophesying death and destruction to God's people. In Jeremiah 31, the prophet speaks of what will lie ahead for God's people if they repent and return to their God.

Read the passage again slowly, as if you were in a dark, doomsday world (or just your everyday world if you're having one of those Hard

Days). Listen to Jeremiah's words as if he were standing on a hill above you, his tired, wrinkled face awash in peace and hope and glory with these words. How would you paraphrase his words for your life today?

_____

_____

_____

Pray, "Father, show me what You want me to learn in this passage." Now reread the verses and finish this sentence: God wants me to...

_____

_____

_____

My Prayer

_____

_____

_____

48

Pooh Bear or Spider-Man?

So come on, let's leave the preschool fingerpainting exercises on Christ and get on with the grand work of art. Grow up in Christ. The basic foundational truths are in place: turning your back on "salvation by self-help" and turning in trust toward God; baptismal instructions; laying on of hands; resurrection of the dead; eternal judgment. God helping us, we'll stay true to all that. But there's so much more. Let's get on with it!
HEBREWS 6:1–3

Jack and Olivia and I went to the store yesterday to buy last-minute supplies for Jack's three-year-old birthday party. At the cash register, Olivia offered to buy Jack a Mylar balloon as a gift. I nudged him toward the Winnie-the-Pooh head—a balloon as big as the Hindenburg. I'd just scratched four walls of nursery room paper off his bedroom, making way for lizards and frogs and dinosaurs, and was feeling a bit nostalgic, I guess.

But Jack wouldn't go for it. He wanted Spider-Man. He's all about the superheroes these days—refusing

Things on My Mind

Concerns, to-do lists, grocery lists, whatever—get these things down here so you can concentrate for the next ten minutes.

_____

_____

_____

_____

Nemo undies in favor of Batman. His favorite gift from the party? A Batman cape I bought at Wal-Mart for $3.88.

Jack is moving on. I'm as melancholy as I was when we boxed up his last bottle and sent it to Goodwill. He's not quite ready for the Spider-Man movie—it's a bit too complicated for him to follow—but he knows what he's drawn to. He wants a challenge, not the same old thing.

It got me thinking about adults and how we get into one favorite thing and never break out of it. I just read that if you're coasting, you're actually going slightly downhill. And yet we coast with the same friends, the same church, the same level of Bible study (or no Bible study at all), the same prayer life, the same memorized scriptures, the same understanding of God.

I'm not advocating switching over to the new Church of What's Happening Now. Never committing to a church, a faith home, doesn't benefit anyone. I'm just saying that we need to constantly seek the next challenge in our lives if we want to grow, if we want to know who God wants us to ultimately be.

We can do that by listening to new songwriters, reading new books, listening to people on the radio whom we respect and who challenge our thinking. We can seek out new friends, people we truly admire and want to emulate. We can enroll in a Bible study that we secretly fear is over our heads and trust that God will make up the difference.

God calls us to the mountains, which means there's a hike ahead. He never says, "Go and coast along. You're just fine." Certainly there are times in our lives when we simply need to rest or to absorb what we just learned. But then we need to get moving again.

So where are you? Are you in a comfortable Hundred Acre Wood spot, knowing Piglet or Tigger or Christopher Robin is about to stop by? Or are you taking on the world with Spider-Man, fighting the bad guys, trying to make peace, and seeking some understanding of how God made you and why?

God, I'm asking for the heart of Spider-Man, for the courage to swing out there on a narrow thread, trusting You. I ask You to help me fight evil in this world and not run back to my cozy home and ignore the fights. I want to be brave, a warrior for You. I want to learn all You have to teach me. And I trust that if I put myself out there, You won't let me make a total fool of myself. I trust that You'll honor the effort and risk. Make me courageous, Father, in everything I do, every day of my life. Amen.

What Is God Saying to Me in This?

_____

_____

_____

Making the Scripture Mine

In Hebrews 6:1–3, the author is addressing spiritual lethargy, taking Hebrew Christians to task for embracing their faith and then slowly backsliding to the basics again. This is very relevant to today's Christians—to you and me. So often we have moments where we gain special insight and experience spiritual growth, but then we let it go in the midst of *life*. We forget what we're to be about—growing ever closer to Christ.

Read the passage again slowly, as if your own spiritual advisor has taken you to a quiet corner of the room to give you her insight on your spiritual life. How would you reword the message for your life today?

_____

_____

_____

Pray, "Father, show me what You want me to learn in this passage." Now reread the verses and finish this sentence: God wants me to…

_____

_____

_____

My Prayer

_____

_____

_____

49

She Warrior

In the same way I was with Moses, I'll be with you. I won't give up on you; I won't leave you. Strength! Courage!… Give it everything you have, heart and soul.… Don't get off track, either left or right, so as to make sure you get to where you're going. And don't for a minute let this Book of The Revelation be out of mind. Ponder and meditate on it day and night, making sure you practice everything written in it. Then you'll get where you're going; then you'll succeed. Haven't I commanded you? Strength! Courage! Don't be timid; don't get discouraged. GOD, your God, is with you every step you take.

JOSHUA 1:5–9

Things on My Mind

Concerns, to-do lists, grocery lists, whatever—get these things down here so you can concentrate for the next ten minutes.

_____

_____

_____

Last week I was convinced that we were not going to make our mortgage payments for more than another month; that I would never get a contracted book outlined, much less written; that I wasn't doing a good job as a wife or mother; and, oh yes, that my husband was going to die on the road and we didn't have enough life insurance on him. How's that for a general attack from Satan? Sadly, I wasn't much of a She Warrior. I was depressed and discouraged, feeling like my life was in a terrible whirlpool. Next stop: bottom.

My friend Rebecca called me and talked to me, prayed me through it. I can always count on her to remind me that, while specific concerns can be from the Holy Spirit to inspire change, general attacks are usually from the devil. Been there yourself? Repeat after me: "General attacks—Satan. Specific concerns—Spirit." Pay attention. Who is turning your head?

Joshua 1:5 tells us that God will always be with us and, more importantly, that He will never fail us. What a blessed assurance! Pastor and author Rick Warren says, "If you are giving into fear, then you have quit believing God." Whoa. Every time I think of that, I find it convicting—and assuring too. He's right; if we believe in the God who promises *to never leave us or fail us,* then fear has no place in our lives! And yet we doubt! We actively proclaim disbelief rather than powerful faith!

So I'm working on becoming a She Warrior. I admit I'm still in training and probably will be all my life. But I know where I want to be. I know *who* I want to be. I want to be Strong and Heroic in my faith. I want to be constantly Encouraged, not giving into discouragement. I want to be on the front lines with the sword of truth (the Word) in my hands and the shield of faith guarding my body and soul. I want to be living with the blessed assurance that every step I take, God is with me. Join me, friends. We're on the front lines whether we recognize it or not. Will you be run over or take on the fight with God at your side?

Father God, I am weak. Sometimes I feel nothing like a warrior. I feel like a little girl cowering in fear. Forgive me for times when I do not step out in faith. Forgive me for times when I give in to panic and discouragement. Protect me and keep me in Your tender care. Thank You for always walking with me, Lord. Help me keep my eyes on You. Amen.

What Is God Saying to Me in This?

_____

_____

_____

Making the Scripture Mine

One of the toughest aspects of the book of Joshua is that God calls His people to holy war, to what Peterson translates as "holy curse." God tells His people to move into the land of Canaan and leave no survivors. We have to remember what the inhabitants were like, however. They had "a snake pit of child sacrifice and sacred prostitution," as Peterson describes it. Suddenly we recognize warriors of light in a land of darkness. Thankfully, we are not called to kill, but we are called to battle back the dark, here and now.

Read Joshua 1:5–9 again slowly, as if a military leader was shouting the words to you and your comrades. How would you word the message for your life today?

_____

_____

_____

Pray, "Father, show me what You want me to learn in this passage." Now reread the verses and finish this sentence: God wants me to...

_____

_____

_____

My Prayer

_____

_____

_____

_____

_____

_____

50

Sleeping Through the Call

Why do you confuse the issue?
Why do you talk without knowing what you're talking about?
Pull yourself together, Job!
Up on your feet! Stand tall!
I have some questions for you,
and I want some straight answers.
Where were you when I created the earth?
Tell me, since you know so much!
Who decided on its size? Certainly you'll know that!
Who came up with the blueprints and measurements?
How was its foundation poured,
and who set the cornerstone,
While the morning stars sang in
    chorus
and all the angels shouted praise?
                    JOB 38:2–7

Things on My Mind

Concerns, to-do lists, grocery lists, whatever—get these things down here so you can concentrate for the next ten minutes.

I was in Alaska on one of those rare occasions that I had to leave my family and have an adventure...all by myself. I'd come in from a day flying above tundra and moose, landing on tiny ponds at fourteen thousand feet, and interviewing bush families for a novel I was writing. Cool, eh? But I was crushed when I returned to the inn to find out that, the night before, I'd missed the glorious northern lights.

The front desk clerk offered to call me if they came out again, and I jumped at the chance. Sure enough, at 1:30 AM she called and said, "Ms. Bergren, your northern lights are out."

I threw on my clothes and raced outside, one of perhaps twenty who emerged from the inn of slumber to gaze upward in awe. As a three-quarter moon shone over our right shoulders, the entire Alaskan range glowed an eerie white against a dark sky. A silver, glittering river wound across the valley floor. And the lights... They were everything you hear about the aurora borealis—dancing, neon green and crimson red—and at the last, they were shooting down toward us as if angel wings were covering, covering, covering us.

To my left, a man said, never looking away, "I've been to Denali ten years running, and this is the first time I've seen Mount McKinley, let alone the northern lights." To my right, another said, "I've lived in Alaska for forty years, and I've never seen northern lights like this." And I was there for a weekend. A weekend.

I stood with face turned upward, weeping, weeping for the gracious-ness of God. It was a miraculous moment, an experience I'll never forget, watching the Master Weaver at His work, tying light to light. Reaching out to cover His children.

And I could've missed it. I could've slept through it. When the clerk called me, I glanced out my window, and it was a tiny green wave in the distance. By the time I got downstairs and went outside, it was a full-blown angel dance above us. I could've rolled over and gone to sleep, dis-missing the light as not a big deal, and missed the best northern lights a native Alaskan had seen in forty years.

What are we missing every day? What are we sleeping through? We must stay vigilant, be God-watchers day in and day out. Our babies absorb so much. When did we quit absorbing, quit observing with awe, the King's creation all about us?

Father, forgive me for getting into the day to day of my life and forgetting the miracle of Your handiwork all about me. Shake me awake! Slap my cheeks! Open my eyes! Make me see You and Your glory each and every day! Amen!

What Is God Saying to Me in This?

_____

_____

_____

Making the Scripture Mine

I feel sorry for Job when I read Job 38:2–7. He's been through the wringer, tested by God in the face of everything the devil can throw at him: loss of family, home, wealth, health. And God comes after him in a forthright way, like a frustrated father in the face of a spoiled child. *Remember where you came from. You came from Me. Everything comes from Me. Trust Me.*

Read the passage again slowly, as if you were listening to God speak to you from a burning bush or a whirling tornado. How would you word the message for your life today?

_____

_____

_____

Pray, "Father, show me what You want me to learn in this passage." Now reread the verses and finish this sentence: God wants me to…

_____

_____

_____

My Prayer

_____

_____

_____

_____

_____

_____

51

Mean Girls

Do you think anyone is going to be able to drive a wedge between us and Christ's love for us? There is no way! Not trouble, not hard times, not hatred, not hunger, not homelessness, not bullying threats, not backstabbing, not even the worst sins listed in Scripture.... None of this fazes us because Jesus loves us. I'm absolutely convinced that nothing—nothing living or dead, angelic or demonic, today or tomorrow, high or low, thinkable or unthinkable—absolutely *nothing* can get between us and God's love because of the way that Jesus our Master has embraced us.

ROMANS 8:35–39

Things on My Mind

Concerns, to-do lists, grocery lists, whatever—get these things down here so you can concentrate for the next ten minutes.

_____

_____

_____

I'm always amazed at how mean girls can be to one another. Olivia, my middle schooler, is at odds with a girl who sits at her lunch table, a girl who seems to be very jealous of Olivia's best friendship with Hannah. She'd prefer to be Hannah's best friend. I've coached Olivia over the last year and a half on how to deal with this girl, how to maintain her calm, how to continue to be nice and friendly without going overboard. But yesterday Liv came home in tears. Mean Girl had passed out invitations to her slumber party at the lunch table, in front of Olivia, to everyone but her. Then Mean Girl stared at Olivia, waiting for her to react or break down.

Boy, it's tough not to go down to that school and talk to Mean Girl myself, to call her mother and ask her if she knows how her daughter is acting. I'd like to resolve it. But this is a critical task before my daughter now. She must be able to deal with this girl and to stand up for herself while maintaining a sense of peace and love.

Inside, I want to throttle the venomous little viper, but I dig deep, looking for the mothering words of guidance Olivia needs rather than my Mother Bear wrath. I tell Liv to concentrate on the good friends she does have. I tell her Mean Girl must be jealous and not to let Mean Girl get to her, because that's just what Mean Girl wants. I remind Olivia that she can stand up for herself and call Mean Girl on action that is out of line but to keep it out of the personal arena. "When she is unkind, Liv, call her on it. Tell her it's uncool. When you smile at her, and she doesn't smile back, ask her why. Ask her what the obstacle is for her…"

This is grown-up stuff, hard even for those of us who have seen the last of our twenties and thirties. But this is primary for us all. Jesus would deal with said Mean Girl in truth and love. This is what we're called to do too. Talk to her about her mean actions; make her pay attention. Love her with grace. See her the way God sees her—perhaps lonely, perhaps sad inside, perhaps needing something we could supply if we could get past the mean, outer crust. Pray for her.

While most of us aren't so overtly mean, all of us are occasionally Mean Girls. We pass up the opportunity to help one another; we turn away from a friend in need because we're too absorbed with our own lives; we say cutting things in our minds even if they don't come out of our mouths; we shove down an encouraging word because another's need makes us feel superior; we judge our sisters… The list goes on and on.

But my daughter is trying not to fall into the Mean Girl trap. So am I. And someday the Mean Girls we encounter will not affect us. We will nod at them with grace and love and keep on walking—no tears, no struggle, just peace that God sees it all and celebrates us.

Father, pulverize every mean bone in my body. Make me a vessel of love who reaches out to others with grace and peace. Help me see those who mistreat me with Your eyes of love, as if I had x-ray vision to see why they act wrongly and how they are still Your special children. Make me a Grace Girl, Jesus. In Your holy name. Amen.

What Is God Saying to Me in This?

_____

_____

_____

Making the Scripture Mine

Eugene Peterson calls Romans "a piece of exuberant and passionate thinking." He goes on to say, "Paul takes the well-witnessed and devoutly believed fact of the life, death, and resurrection of Jesus of Nazareth and thinks through its implications."[8] In Romans 8:35–39, Paul refers to the fact that Jesus Himself, who died for us, now lives at the right hand of God, in the position of power, and intercedes for us. Nothing we can do and nothing that life throws at us can get in the way of that.

Consider for a moment that you think you've done something that would keep you from Christ's love and acceptance and protection…and that you've dared to tell the apostle Paul. Reread the passage as if he's speaking to you right now, wherever you are. Can you see his face, desperate that you understand the truth at last? What words from the scripture speak most to you today?

_____

_____

_____

Pray, "Father, show me what You want me to learn in this passage." Now reread the verses and finish this sentence: God wants me to…

_____

_____

_____

My Prayer

_____

_____

_____

52

Out with the Old, In with the New

For a child has been born—for us!
the gift of a son—for us!
He'll take over
the running of the world.
His names will be: Amazing Counselor,
Strong God,
Eternal Father,
Prince of Wholeness.
                —ISAIAH 9:6

Things on My Mind

Concerns, to-do lists, grocery lists, whatever—get these things down here so you can concentrate for the next ten minutes.

_____

_____

_____

_____

And so here we are again…just around the corner, a brand-new year. New hope, new opportunities. Dreams of being a better mom, a better wife, a better friend, a better disciple.

I'm an optimistic person, but even I know that all my good intentions will fade within weeks, if not days. But remember that God holds tightly to the New Year dream, even when we give up on it. He sees us with all the tenderness and hope that a mother sees in her own child, as we see in the Christ child, born to us.

If we could hold on to His vision, His hope, His dreams for us, it would fuel our fire all year long. If we could just hold on to the joy of that candlelit Christmas Eve service, when we tear up at the thought of *seeing* the Baby Jesus, holding the squalling, waving Christ in our arms, knowing He would have come for us alone and that He loves us just the way we are now… If we could retain that focus all year long, it would keep our goals for change and progress and *life* in order.

So as I strive to be a better wife, mother, friend, disciple, I will remember to first keep my biggest resolution of all—to hold the Prince of Wholeness in my arms and close to my heart every day. He's the only one who will understand every time I miss the mark but also will never fail to encourage me onward. After all, this Baby, not us, is the One who came to take over the running of our world. In Him and through Him, we can make the greatest resolutions of all.

Here's to the new year…and beyond!

Dear Jesus, thank You for loving me just the way I am: imperfect, sinful, unlovable at times. Cleanse my heart and make me new every morning of this new year. Show me how I can grow to be a better servant in You, one baby goal at a time. Amen.

What Is God Saying to Me in This?

_____

_____

_____

Making the Scripture Mine

The names for Jesus in Isaiah 9:6 are called the four royal-throne names of the Messiah—Wonderful Counselor, Mighty God, Everlasting Father, and Prince of Peace. Peterson translates them as "Amazing Counselor, Strong God, Eternal Father, Prince of Wholeness." My *NIV Study Bible* says of

"Wonderful Counselor": the "Son of David will carry out...'marvelous things, things planned long ago.'" It says of "Mighty God": "His divine power as a warrior is stressed." Of "Everlasting Father": "He will be an enduring, compassionate provider and protector." And of "Prince of Peace": "His rule will bring wholeness and well-being to individuals and to society."[9]

This is the Baby of babies. Come for me. Come for you. Coming again for all of us.

Read the verse again slowly, as if you were watching Isaiah's face, alight with vision and glory. How would you rephrase the scripture for your life today? What would you call the Messiah?

_____

_____

Pray, "Father, show me what You want me to learn in this passage." Now reread the verse and finish this sentence: God wants me to...

_____

_____

_____

My Prayer

_____

_____

_____

Acknowledgments

Heartfelt thanks are in order to many who helped me get this book done. First, my family, who continually gave me (and still gives me) the means to see how God is alive and well and working constantly in all our lives. More than anything else in my experience, parenting has taught me how my God loves, cares, protects, and guides me. My family graciously allowed me to use all our experiences as the cloth on which I would embroider this book. My friends, especially Sarah and Rebecca, became adept at saying, "There's a devotional in that!"—helping me see how God was at work everywhere I looked. And my editors, Jeanette Thomason, Carol Bartley, and Lisa Guest, did a great job in putting this book into presentable form. Special thanks also to Steve Laube, my agent, and Steve Cobb, trusted friend and publisher. I remain in debt to you all.

Notes

1. Eugene Peterson, "Introduction to 1 John," *The Message: The Bible in Contemporary Language* (Colorado Springs, CO: NavPress, 2002), 2222.
2. Kenneth Barker, gen. ed., *The NIV Study Bible, New International Version* (Grand Rapids: Zondervan, 1985), note on Deuteronomy 30:20.
3. Barker, *The NIV Study Bible*, note on 1 Peter 2:2.
4. Barker, *The NIV Study Bible*, note on Psalm 34:15–18.
5. Peterson, "Introduction to 1–2 Peter," *The Message*, 2209.
6. Barker, *The NIV Study Bible*, note on 2 Corinthians 12:9.
7. Peterson, "Introduction to Matthew," *The Message*, 1743.
8. Peterson, "Introduction to Romans," *The Message*, 2030.
9. Barker, *The NIV Study Bible*, note on Isaiah 9:6.

Topical Index

Scripture Index

About the Author

LISA T. BERGREN is the award-winning, best-selling author of twenty-two books with more than 1.2 million copies sold, including *The Begotten* and *The Betrayed, The Bridge, Christmas Every Morning,* the Northern Lights series, the Full Circle series, and her popular and acclaimed children's picture books: *God Gave Us You, God Gave Us Two,* and *God Gave Us Christmas.* Lisa is a wife to Tim, mother of three children, a businesswoman involved in several companies, a Bible-study leader, and an avid reader. The Bergrens reside in Colorado Springs, Colorado. To receive free devotionals via e-mail and to learn more about her, please visit her online at www.LisaTawnBergren.com.

•••••

To learn about Lisa's new Bible study for women, *What Women Want* (written with her good friend Rebecca Price), go to www.SatisfiedHeart.com. There you can find personal and group retreat guides, download music, read interviews with today's Christian leaders, and more!